Sherlock
Being
Catfished

A Memoir

JOAN MELLEN

Published by:
Trine Day LLC
PO Box 577
Walterville, OR 97489
1-800-556-2012
www.TrineDay.com
TrineDay@icloud.com

Library of Congress Control Number: 2024933167

Mellen, Joan
–1st ed.
p. cm.

Epub (ISBN-13): 978-1-63424-484-8
Trade Paperback (ISBN-13): 978-1-63424-483-1
1. Autobiography. 2. Joan Mellen. 3. Man-woman relationships. 4.
Facebook. 5. Kennedy, John F. 1917-1963 Assassination. I. Mellen, Joan. II. Title

FIRST EDITION
10 9 8 7 6 5 4 3 2 1

Printed in the USA
Distribution to the Trade by:
Independent Publishers Group (IPG)
814 North Franklin Street
Chicago, Illinois 60610
312.337.0747
www.ipgbook.com

PUBLISHER'S FOREWORD

Love oh love, Oh careless love
Love oh love, Oh careless love
You robbed me, Out of my silver
You robbed me, Out of my gold
I'll be damned, If I let you
Rob me out of my soul
                    – Traditional

I'll give you jewelery and money, too
That ain't all, that ain't all I'll do for you
Oh, if you bring it to me
Bring your sweet loving
Bring it on home to me
Yeah (yeah) yeah (yeah) yeah (yeah)
                    – Sam Cooke, 1962

The old saw by Heraclitus, *The Only Constant In Life Is Change*, is definitely getting its workout these days. Welcome to 2024...
The game's afoot!
I find it interesting that the concept of "paradigm shift" presented by Thomas Kuhn in his book, *The Structure of Scientific Revolutions,* was published in 1962, a year before the nation-numbing assassination that continues to extract a toll on generations of Americans ... and the world at large.

The trauma, deceit and disarray of that day lingers yet across our corrupted body-politic, stilted economic fortunes, and dysfunctional social malaise. A perfidy visited upon us through more than simple fate, but, rather, conspiratorial activity.

Joan Mellen addressed this "evil" by authoring the definitive account of Jim Garrison and his quest to find the murderers.

In her memoir, *Sherlock, Being Catfished* Joan bravely and courageously tells her own tale of being hornswoggled by one of our newfangled nefarious undercurrents. She also recounts various tidbits of information and vignettes from years of exploring the JFK assassination, Jim Garrison, and her personal interactions with the various players within the JFK assassination research community.

We also learn much besides, as Joan has done more than write about New Orleans District Attorney Garrison and his investigations into the machinations of the killing of our President. She shares her lifelong interests in movies, culture, politics, and sports. Joan lets us into her personal and professional lives.

SHERLOCK BEING CATFISHED: A MEMOIR is a brutally honest narrative – defiantly told. TrineDay is proud and honored to publish this fearless retort.

Who among us likes to be led down the garden path by those looking to take advantage of our humanity?

Hasn't it happened already too often?

The Internet has brought us a new realm of possibilities along with many of the pitfalls of the past.

Personally, I sense we are experiencing a paradigm shift. A revolution of the way of thinking, as bespoke by Kant. Leaving behind the old ways of prevarication, ushering an honest chance to create a better world for our children.

We all live together … whether we like it or not….

> *Heraclitus, I believe, says that all things pass and nothing stays, and comparing existing things to the flow of a river, he says you could not step twice into the same river.*
> – Plato

Onward to the Utmost of Futures,
Peace,
Kris Millegan
Publisher
TrineDay
4/20/24

This book is dedicated to Audrey Szepinski, with gratitude.

BOOKS BY JOAN MELLEN

SHERLOCK BEING CATFISHED: A MEMOIR (2024)

BLOOD IN THE WATER: HOW THE US AND ISRAEL CONSPIRED TO AMBUSH THE USS LIBERTY (2018)

THE GREAT GAME IN CUBA: CIA AND THE CUBAN REVOLUTION (2016)

FAUSTIAN BARGAINS: LYNDON JOHNSON AND MAC WALLACE IN THE ROBBER BARON CULTURE OF TEXAS (2016)

OUR MAN IN HAITI: GEORGE DE MOHRENSCHILDT AND THE CIA IN THE NIGHTMARE REPUBLIC (2012)

JIM GARRISON, HIS LIFE AND TIMES: THE EARLY YEARS. (2008)

MODERN TIMES (2006)

A FAREWELL TO JUSTICE: JIM GARRISON, JFK'S ASSASSINATION AND THE CASE THAT SHOULD HAVE CHANGED HISTORY, (2005) REVISED EDITION (2013)

IN THE REALM OF THE SENSES (2004)

SEVEN SAMURAI (2002; REVISED, REISSUE 2022)

LITERARY MASTERPIECES: ONE HUNDRED YEARS OF SOLITUDE. (2000)

LITERARY MASTERS: GABRIEL GARCÍA MÁRQUEZ (2000)

LITERARY TOPICS: MAGIC REALISM (2000)

HELLMAN AND HAMMETT: THE LEGENDARY PASSION OF LILLIAN HELLMAN AND DASHIELL HAMMETT (1996)

KAY BOYLE: AUTHOR OF HERSELF (1994)

BOB KNIGHT: HIS OWN MAN (1988)

NATURAL TENDENCIES: A NOVEL (1982)

PRIVILEGE: THE ENIGMA OF SASHA BRUCE (1982)

ED. THE WORLD OF LUIS BUÑUEL (1978)

BIG BAD WOLVES: MASCULINITY IN THE AMERICAN FILM (1977)

THE WAVES AT GENJI'S DOOR: JAPAN THROUGH ITS CINEMA (1976)

VOICES FROM THE JAPANESE CINEMA (1975)

WOMEN AND THEIR SEXUALITY IN THE NEW FILM (1973)

MARILYN MONROE (1973)

FILMGUIDE TO THE BATTLE OF ALGIERS (1973)

CONTENTS

Press on, nothing in the world can take the place of persistence. Talent will not; nothing is more common than unsuccessful men with talent. Genius will not; unrewarded genius is almost a proverb [truism]. And education will not; the world is full of educated derelicts. Persistence and determination alone are omnipotent.
                                                              – Calvin Coolidge

FOREWORD

By Maryalice Yakutchik

Caution is not a word that many would associate with Joan Mellen. As an author and university professor, her writing and teaching careers, both many decades long, exemplified the merits of risk-taking to her readers, students, among whom I am numbered, and colleagues.

No matter how vexing the pursuit of truth, or unpopular its telling, Joan was not one to flinch in the face of the nemeses of nonfiction.

Then, recently, *she was catfished*. Duped by a shoddy romance scam. Friends warned her, of course. So did her bank balk when the "man" who was pledging love shared news of a business catastrophe in Cuba and asked her to wire thousands of dollars to a female associate in Vegas.

How, you might wonder, could someone who routinely cut through red tape and lies of government entities and operatives – not to mention the sad excuses of grad students – buy into such an egregious fiction?

Why was Joan so eager to believe? So willing to give of herself, her money, her time, her future?

Those are hard questions. The role that Joan herself played in being catfished exposes a harrowing vulnerability that left her gulping for breath and spiraling down – before it inspired her to write.

In her brutal retelling, this cautionary tale is fresh. In examining herself, Joan mines an extraordinary character in the context of an unsavory subject. It was her habit as an author of biographies and history to imagine herself as others, if not to obliterate herself entirely.

She was not of interest to herself. It was never about her. Until now.

In these pages, readers will meet a generous and indomitable human spirit whose lifelong project was concealing herself. As if that's not enough, she bears witness to a terrifying global phenomenon of deceit that has momentum and the power to wilt souls.

Thanks to Mellen's honesty, we emerge fortified, no longer available for the taking by catfishers nor anyone else.

Maryalice Yakutchik, a career science journalist, was a student of Joan Mellen's in the creative writing program at Temple University. Her work has appeared across the Discovery Channel, NPR, the Philadelphia Inquirer, and many other outlets.

INTRODUCTION

Now and then, over the years when I dwelled in the realm of Kennedy assassination research, strangers would want to know why I did not reply to their Facebook messages. These communiques included questions they assumed I could answer if only I chose to. The subtext was that there must be something very wrong with me. Or else time had passed me by, and not in a favorable way. Hostility to Facebook could only mean lack of relevancy.

Early in my career as a writer, I had decided to write a biography of Jim Garrison, who believed that the CIA had some role in the murder of John F. Kennedy. Surely, these inquiring minds concluded, the Agency must have broken into my house, stolen files, hacked into my computer. As far as I knew, it had not.

I had run into a few CIA-connected types. Among them was a dashing soldier of fortune, Cuban operations, named Gerald Patrick Hemming. Gerry sported two uncles who were "friends" of CIA counter-intelligence Chief James Angleton. On the day in 1999 when I met Hemming at his home in Fayetteville, North Carolina, a few miles from Fort Bragg, he solemnly advised me to

Hemming

buy the most expensive security system that I could afford.

Hemming's reputation was for physical violence, and that he could fire machine guns simultaneously from both hips. He was a witness I feared. I asked a CIA contract pilot named

Carl McNabb whether I would be in physical danger should I meet with Hemming alone. McNabb laughed.

At the address Hemming had shared with me was a small one-story house. Inside was a rangy man at least six feet seven inches tall. His muscles had gone slack, but his voice remained rich in bravado. Bored, disabled from a heart ailment, and housebound, he retained a gleam in his eye. He had watched a documentary in which I had been interviewed about detective story master, Dashiell Hammett, author of *The Maltese Falcon*, and he had liked it. So he agreed to this meeting.

Hemming's mode of discourse was to test people by mixing truth with disinformation. He declared that of all the people connected to the Kennedy assassination, the one he feared most was "Bernie."

"Bernie? Bernie who?"

"Just Bernie," he said, and the subject was closed.

It would be years before he would tell me whom he was talking about, Bernardo de Torres Alvarez. Many writers avoided Hemming because he had rendered himself an unreliable witness. How could I – how could anyone – distinguish between what was true and what was invention? That I had never heard of Bernie led me to conclude that this was sheer fantasy. I turned out to be wrong.

Hemming had another side, of course. His sheer zest for life and wit made him fun to be with. He told me that during his incarceration for drug trafficking he learned to cook pork fried rice. When I visited, he stood at the stove creating his specialty. Then he did the dishes. He was funny, outrageous, and

Sylvia Odio

not at all threatening. When he talked about his pursuit of a JFK witness named Sylvia Odio, well-known to researchers, he was even sexy.

"Name a figure whom you admire," he said. I chose the figure I hoped would be the subject of my next book, Colombian priest Camilo Torres Restrepo, who had left the priesthood to join the ELN only soon to be murdered, betrayed by the leader of the guerrilla group. Hemming claimed to know who Camilo was. He told me he had learned a lot about Colombia when he had been imprisoned at Gorgona off the Western coast of Colombia. Bats hung from the cement walls and when you dared venture outside snakes slithered at your feet (hence the name Gorgona Island).

If you conclude that all this was more Hemming fantasy, you would be wrong. Years later at dinner in Miami with Hemming's closest friend, aviator Howard K. Davis, or "Davy," – as Hemming called him – told me that they had been on a humanitarian mission in Central America only for Hemming suddenly to disappear. He was found to be drug trafficking. Then, at Hemming's memorial service, his brother Robert confirmed that Gerry had been imprisoned on Gorgona Island which until 1982 had been an active prison for drug traffickers.

* * *

My standard response to all intimidation attempts meant to frighten me because of my study of the intelligence services was inspired by Jim Garrison himself. He was expressing his astonishment at Bobby Kennedy's open hostility to his efforts to expose who had murdered his brother.

As soon as you learn something, Garrison said, shout it from the rooftops. Only this will keep you safe. Your antagonists will have nothing more to fear from you. Had Bobby Kennedy revealed what he knew about the circumstances of his brother's death, and no one doubts that he knew a lot, at the least he might have saved his own life.

To square the circle, Hemming was a Garrison suspect for a while. When Hemming offered boldly to join his investigation, Garrison turned him down, unimpressed by Hemming's clever doubletalk. He penetrated the smoke that Hemming sent his way in the form of a long list of suspects, none of whom had anything to do with the assassination. Coincidentally, they all emanated from the West Coast.

Running for the presidency in 2023, Bobby's son and namesake did not believe it worthwhile to ask me what I knew about his father's relationship to the Garrison investigation. Nor did I value talking to the anti-vaxxer. Not wanting to know the facts about an unsavory historical event was a familiar response from people curious about the assassinations of the 1960s but not open to facts. By our time, draped across several generations, this narrow mindedness had grown to epidemic proportions. Robert F. Kennedy Jr. was ready to trade on the Kennedy name, for what it was worth, but apparently had no interest in knowing what the Kennedys were actually about. I tried to interview one of his sisters, Kerry Kennedy, but when the word "Cuba" came up, she terminated the call. As many of the Miami Cubans well knew, Bobby was implicated in attempts to murder Fidel Castro, and knew the name "Lee Harvey Oswald." Bobby even had a CIA aide search in Canada for Mafia-connected assassins who might be available to participate in such a scheme to eliminate Castro.

* * *

One day in the early spring of 2023 (for a sense of that soft welcoming season, for which there is no word in English, think of the film *Early Spring* by Japanese film master Yasujiro Ozu), my life ground to a halt.

Sherlock with Orleans Parish District Attorney Jim Garrison, New Orleans, Louisiana, 1969.

Feeling neglected in a research field crowded with men, at loose ends because I had just retired after 50 years of university teaching, I unearthed from the moldy attic of Facebook a batch of unanswered messages. Nearly all were from men with queries about Garrison and the JFK assassination. Some invited me to appear on their podcasts or in documentary films whose shelf life had come and gone.

At first, I did not notice that among these messages was one that had nothing to do with Garrison or the Kennedy assassination. I had no idea that I had entered a world that is commonly known as "catfishing," or that $15,000 of my money would soon be in jeopardy.

Sherlock with New Zealand novelist Maurice Shadbolt, Toronto, Canada, circa 1999.

Sherlock with novelist Samuel R. (Chip) Delany, New York City, 2006, at the book party for "A Farewell to Justice," at the Century Association.

I

HOOKERS

The term catfishing derives from the practice of an American fishing village that had been exporting cod to China. The cod were arriving mushy and inedible, although they had been shipped off alive and well. A fisherman came up with the idea of placing catfish in the tank with the cod. On that long journey, catfish nipped at the fins of the cod, keeping them moving and alert, and ensuring that the cod would arrive full of vitality. Without catfish as travel companions, the cod became limp, their flesh unpalatable, and the entire enterprise for naught. Fresh firm catfish were now surviving the long journey to oblivion. Even in the original myth, cruelty suffuses catfishing.

In my analogy, the catfish are the aggressors, often originating on Facebook and other social media sites. Their victims are the cod, the ones catfish exploit. The catfish seek out victims whose lives they attempt to appropriate, and whose money they attempt to steal. The cod, in this analogy, are controlled by the catfish, who find victims not in remote fishing villages, but online. What the human catfish must do is disguise their identities by taking on false names, genders, and backgrounds.

The practice is so widespread that most people from the last two generations know about it. My own research assistant, Audrey, knew all about it. *I had never heard of it.*

Soon unbeknownst to me, if not to Audrey, there already existed a series on the cable network MTV called *Catfish: The TV Show*. Episode after episode encourages the victims to forgive the catfish who created havoc in their lives. The false implication is that these victims have time to start over. When Dashiel Hammett stopped writing, his great friend, Lillian

Hellman, bit her lip. "He acts as if he had all the time in the world," Lily complained. She turned out to be right. Hammett wrote a few fragmentary pieces, but never returned to his elegant form with its incandescent stoicism. The lesson is the same for all of us: we don't have all the time in the world.

From the Netflix documentaries about Manti Te'O (*The Girlfriend Who Didn't Exist*) and *The Tinder Swindler*, and MTV's *Catfish* (now upward of 500 episodes after more than a decade going strong), audiences are increasingly familiar with the dirty business known as catfishing. Men (and to a lesser extent, women) pretend to fall in love with vulnerable individuals, only to rob them of their savings and in the process, destroy their wellbeing, and finally their sanity.

Nev, the host of *Catfish*, is inundated by messages from people begging for help, determined to identify their tormentors. One of the more grotesque stories involves a forty-something woman who catfished her own daughter's 16-year-old boyfriend, using nude photographs of her daughter, some snapped by herself. A decade later she still doesn't perceive the consequences of her deceit. "I'm sorry," she murmurs unconvincingly, "I didn't want to hurt anyone." It's obvious to viewers, if not to Nev, that her quasi-apologies are worthless.

In my ivory-tower life, I never heard of catfishing until I was catfished. My life's work as a nonfiction writer involved intrepid investigation and dogged research. It might have saved me. But it didn't.

In a spin of contradiction. I fell in love in a self-induced hypnosis with the author of one of those unsolicited Facebook messages, even as I am the author of 24 books, all analytic in character. *The Waves at Genji's Door* is a social history of Japan as seen through Japanese cinema. *The Great Game in Cuba* is about CIA's complicated relationship with the Cuban revolution. *Our Man in Haiti* chronicles Papa Doc's regime using documents buried in the archives of military intelligence, extracted through FOIA (Freedom of Information Act) suits.

Sherlock with novelist Ruth Prawer Jhabvala and Cedric Jhabvala at the Century Associa-tion, New York City, 2006, book party for *A Farewell to Justice.*

A Farewell to Justice is a biography of New Orleans DA Jim Garrison and his investigation of the Kennedy assassination, which turned into my own investigation of that subject eight years in the making. That I had known Garrison was a hard-earned benefit, although one truism I experienced was that you had at least to have met your subject to be a decent biographer.

From these titles, you might think that I, having been a long-time professor of non-fiction writing at an urban university, as well as a hard-researching reporter, undeterred by slippery sources and endless FOIA filings, would have developed some level of immunity to romance scams, as they are known. Yet, catfished, I was no wiser than poor Manti, who was the victim of so vicious a scam that his life was ruined. He lost the Heisman trophy and was bounced from NFL first round consideration, losing the millions of dollars that would certainly have come to him from a first round NFL signing. That scam continued for more than a year.

I was no more self-protective than the Tinder addict from Norway who lost several hundred thousand dollars, placing herself in a lifetime of debt. She was beautiful, blond, slen-

11

der and affable, unlike the ugly and slimy catfish that swam into her space.

Many years their senior and professionally experienced in ferreting out surreptitious goings on, I should have known better. But knowing and feeling, intellect and heart were not communicating, leaving me as vulnerable as a 20-year-old. I had retired from teaching and, truth be told, I had time on my hands.

* * *

"Hi, it's me, Michael on Facebook," someone wrote out of the blue. Skeptical, I asked how he knew me. Something doesn't feel right, and I am suspicious. "Michael" has a ready answer. "You popped up under people I may know," he rejoins.

This rejoinder is a daily lure thrown by catfish to Facebook users who are attempting to draw people into their pages. You see a photograph of an interesting person, and you are simultaneously asked to accept or reject this person as a "friend." I could not possibly be a person "Michael," or anyone he knew, might know. But, as I was to discover, Facebook is not accountable to anyone, anywhere, for its questionable algorithmic suggestions. Nor is Facebook alone. Don't forget Instagram, TikTok, Tinder, and who knows what else. One of these sites has the word porn in it.

He lived in Thatcher, Arizona, he said. He was a logger, and his name was "Michael Devlin."

I must have liked him because I gave him my email address.

"I hope you have a wonderful day, Joan." This email is signed "Michael Devlin, Chat @ Spike." I had never heard of "Chat @ Spike." It was Sunday, June 11th. I was not ready to give up on the commas or, as time passed, on Standard English grammar either, although when I taught Remedial English, I was a fierce adherent of correct grammar. Yet I did not receive such cheery emails often. So I took his message at face value.

I want to get closer to him. I tell him that I'm studying my own research about Haiti for a documentary for which I will be interviewed. I tell him that I don't have my books on a computer and ask if that's a problem should he want to read them. He does not address any of this. He skips over to generalities.

He informs me that for the past weeks he has been on a logging assignment in Cuba! He does not volunteer where in Cuba he is based. He says that he starts work at 9:00 AM and will be done by 5:30. "The weather here is delightful," he adds, "I love my job and the smell of the woods." This doesn't sound like Cuba, where in June it's hot and steamy. But how would I know? I've never been there.

"So, I'm assuming you are single?"

To this I don't reply. It doesn't seem that we are connecting. It's only June 14th.

"So, what are your plans today, Joan?" he says. Almost but not quite a non-sequitur.

I am not ready to give up on him.

* * *

The education section of his Facebook profile was blank. The person by whom I was catfished appeared to have never attended college. It might have been a man or a woman who had stolen his identity – I was never to hear "their" voice or even catch a glimpse. Within a month, he or she, or both were begging me for large sums of money. At first light it certainly seemed as if I had no means of defending myself. Already I believed I loved "him," *and that was all that mattered* to me.

A literary analogue appears at the close of Marcel Proust's *In Search of Lost Time* in Swann's obsession with a woman of easy virtue, a woman, he finally allows, who was "not in my style."

Swann comes to his senses only after he has married Odette, circumscribing what remains of his life. Another analogue is Somerset Maugham's *Of Human Bondage.*

Sherlock with author Ellen Currie, Princeton Library, Princeton, New Jersey, 2006.

Sherlock with novelist Mecca Jamilah Sullivan, a former student and now a full professor at Georgetown University, at Barnes & Noble in Rittenhouse Square, Philadelphia, Pennsylvania, 2006.

II

LOGGERS

My story is a cautionary tale for the growing cadre of souls similarly ensnared.

The only logger I have known is a fictional character, the Woodcutter in Japanese director Akira Kurosawa's film, *Rashomon*, set in eighth century Heian Japan.  Three versions of a rape and murder are recounted at a trial. A fourth is provided by a woodcutter who was a witness to the rape and murder by accident, yet who is no more objective, no less self-serving, than the others–rich woman and her samurai husband or the lawless bandit who attacked them and were the actual participants in the event.

Yet it is the Woodcutter who redeems humanity. At a nearby temple, a disillusioned priest has his faith in humanity restored by our shabby, aging Woodcutter, a man old before his time. Some desperate soul has abandoned a baby in the temple courtyard. The Woodcutter reaches to pick up the baby, only for the priest, believing the Woodcutter wants to steal the baby's luxurious garments, the mark of wealth, to push him aside. The priest has absorbed the lesson inculcated by Jim Garrison's chief suspect, David Ferrie, framed on his living room wall, "People are no damn good."

Yet the priest is wrong. The Woodcutter wants to adopt the abandoned baby, not sell its clothes. Out of compassion for the screaming infant, he wants to take him home. "I have six children of my own," the Woodcutter explains to the priest, modestly. "One more wouldn't make it any more difficult." The dialogue that follows is a competition in humility.

"I'm sorry. I shouldn't have said that," the priest begins.

"Oh, you can't afford not to be suspicious of people these days," the Woodcutter says. "I'm the one who ought to be ashamed."

"No, I'm grateful to you," the priest replies. "Because thanks to you, I think I will be able to keep my faith in men." The baby stops crying, the priest holds him out and the Woodcutter takes him into his arms. The Woodcutter and the priest bow to each other now. Class differences have become immaterial in the face of what matters in the world of men.

* * *

Among the more disconcerting experiences of my investigation of the Garrison case was an interview with David Ferrie's best friend and heir, Alvin Beaubouef. Beaubouef arrived at my suite at the Windsor Court Hotel bearing two open glasses filled with a suspicious yellow liquid. "These are Dirty Martinis," Beaubouef said. I had never heard of it. We sat at a large glass-topped table in the sitting room. I tasted my drink, an innocuous substance.

Alvin Beaubouef.

Suddenly, Beaubouef rose from his chair and rushed over to the closed glass doors leading to the bedroom. He pushed them open violently – only to discover that there was no one hiding inside. What he would have done had there been anyone there I cannot imagine. We went on to dinner where he attacked the Windsor Court chef, a German-born master. "There is better food in New Orleans," he said nastily.

Beaubouef exhibited no compassion for anyone. The interview focused on Ferrie's prowess as an aviator, and on his acquaintance with Mafia boss Carlos Marcello, who did not figure in the Kennedy assassination. As for loggers, woodcutters, or lumberjacks, Kurosawa, in this film dating from 1950,

16

concluded that woodcutters have a better chance at human decency than spoiled rich women, or elegant, supercilious samurai with their class superiority and inflated opinions of themselves. Nor did he romanticize the anarchic bandit played by Toshiro Mifune who lacks any ac-

Carlos Marcello

quaintance with generosity of spirit, let alone kindness.

A woodcutter, Kurosawa concludes, is close to the earth. His first instinct is to attend to the needs of others. In *Rashomon*, the woodcutter heals the ragged soul of the disillusioned priest, and herein lies the meaning of the film. That four people offer differing narratives of the same event is a theme that might have appealed to 20th century western audiences, but it does not seem to have particularly interested Kurosawa.

* * *

And now a woodcutter has entered my twenty-first century life.

More photographs sent by Devlin revealed that as the cliché would have it, he was no George Clooney. Nor was he a Clint Eastwood with his breathtaking stoicism. He did bear a resemblance to the recently deceased singer Jimmy Buffett and his countenance might evoke Buffett's irresistible sweetness and joy in life along with a corresponding sensuality.

Devlin seemed robust and self-assured, if not Superman-graceful as in the 1950's Superman short subjects. These always preceded the main feature at the Osceola, the South Bronx movie theatre on St. Ann's Avenue managed by my father when I was a child. For a time, I was mesmerized by Superman and had a poster of George Reeves as Superman on my corner of the bedroom wall.

In one of the photographs he sent, Devlin was accompanied by a shiny Golden Retriever who could snatch your heart in a millisecond. There was a shadow of a frown on the dog's face, but I attributed that to discomfort with the suffocating Arizona weather.

In the single indoor shot, Michael Devlin is standing at a new silver Wolf stove, like the one I have now at home. There is a spatula in his hand, and he seems to be turning a hamburger. This kitchen offers no signs of human habitation other than Devlin himself dressed in a pressed long-sleeved shirt and khaki pants. No utensils are present other than the spatula, no dishes, no pots and pans, no mess. Then we are back outside on the barren landscape where there are no trees, not even a cactus.

Maybe it was Arizona, but it could as easily have been eighth century Japan, or the planet Tralfamadore, a place we have all yearned to visit. "You had to be from Tralfamadore to understand Hitler and his crowd," Kurt Vonnegut explains in *Slaughterhouse-Five*. Billy Pilgrim, Vonnegut's hero, who does manage to get there, has only good things to say about this place inhabited by small green people where he is lodged in a cage and displayed for the edification of the locals in a zoo. "Only on Earth is there any talk about free will," Vonnegut writes. Nor is there any speculation about "why," the cause of anything. Earthlings would do well to "ignore the awful times and concentrate on the good ones" is Tralfamadorian wisdom.

* * *

"Which of my books have you read?" I ask Devlin. "Actually none," he says, unabashed. That I was an author did not impress him.

"Which would you like to read?" I say. He mentions *Blood in the Water*, the story of the 1967 attack in the East Mediterranean on the intelligence ship, the USS *Liberty*. I am puzzled by this choice, since *Blood in the Water* was not widely reviewed or distributed.

"I want to send you a proper book, not an email. I don't even have my books on my computer. I am from the world of hardcover books. Is that a problem?" I say.

"No, not at all," he says and swiftly changes the topic. "Well, been working here since 9:00 AM and it's been a wonderful day, the weather delightful. Probably will be done by 5:30 today."

Sherlock with Dave Lewis, Chief Intelligence Officer of the USS *Liberty* in New Hampshire, 2018

Devlin's profile on Facebook was curiously scanty. "Education" was a blank. Places he had lived: Blank. Profession was logger, the only fact. The guru of *Catfish: The TV Show* comments in one episode: "what you should expect from a Catfish is a blank profile."

Devlin begins to let loose a flood of emails, two or three a day. He never refers to any book I have written, or he has read, or he wishes to read. I am not offended. Maybe I wrote to him out of longing for more contact with the outside world now that I had retired from teaching. I had no idea of the price of such an adventure. It didn't occur to me that there was a price tag for worldly experience. *Trust me, there is.*

I must have been charmed because I wrote that his dog had the same smile that he had. He enjoyed that and so volunteered that the dog's name was "Reagan." So proceeded my self-censorship. I did not admit that I had never voted for Ronald Reagan. None of my friends or colleagues were Reagan Republicans and in the more than 75 emails to come, Reagan the politician is never mentioned by either of us.

Nor did I explore the political implications of that name. It occurred to me that as a logger, and a man with no apparent formal education, he might for all I knew even be a member of a Trump militia group, the Proud Boys, or the Oath Keepers. This too was a subject I decided I better not address.

Sherlock at event at Books and Books in Coral Gables, Florida, 2005

Sherlock with Gordon Winslow, City of Miami Archivist, 2006

III

WRITERS

On assignment in Cuba, he does not offer any political impressions of the country. The name Fidel Castro does not arise. I ignore a little voice in my head that cautions me that when you are dealing with Internet acquaintances, there are never too many questions. For years I have been contemptuous of people who didn't much care who murdered John F. Kennedy, my potential readers. Was I any better in not holding Devlin's feet to the fire?

I tell him that I have written a book about Cuba. This revelation falls into a black hole. He does seem to assume that his being in Cuba precludes his telephoning me. He invokes the unreliability of his Internet service.

In none of his emails does he use the word telephone. I have fallen into a world that is post-Alexander Graham Bell. If the man won't phone or video chat, *Catfish* host Nev says, "It's not HIM." Catfishing is replete with people, both catfish and their victims, on whom no one can count.

Devlin does try to persuade me to give up emailing in favor of Google Chat, but when I try and fail to accomplish this task, he gives up. *I have never heard of Google Chat.* "Can you send a screenshot of what you find difficult to sign in so I can tutor you on how to go about it?" he asks.

I don't know what a screenshot is.

At this point Devlin gives up.

As for me, I am finding that this use of email is a means of avoiding communication, not fostering it. Should your correspondent refer to something inconvenient, simply ignore it and it will vanish from reality. You, the hopeful recipient, who invoked the unwelcome fact, or observation, are check-mated. You have no choice or free will in the matter, having forfeited the opportunity that only face-to-face contact affords.

The "metaverse" (is this a word?) of the Internet is primitive, despite the folderol of techtalk. It is more silent than not and evinces no affection for the truth. It grants no priority to what actually happened. Truth is its unacknowledged enemy as it flaunts its nihilism in a reflexive postmodern distaste for historical reality. As a biographer, I have long been an adversary of this world view.

The next two weeks welcomes an onslaught of two or three emails a day. I am experiencing a strange renewal. Only a cliché serves. I feel as if an aching weight has been lifted from my shoulders. I am untroubled. Dare I enlist a word that has never been part of my vocabulary? I am "happy." Each day, I wake up earlier, sometimes at 1:30 AM. In the dark I reach for my cell phone to check if there is a new email from Devlin. And often there is.

He begins to address me as "Sunshine." What for many would be commonplace for me is unique. I do not have a sunny personality, not even on the Internet where disguise and fraud are ubiquitous. I have been moody and sad since the day I was born, my mother having refused to take the advice of her practical-minded older sister, Rosalie, and leave my abusive father.

But Devlin's word is now law. I must be Sunshine. I am happy to turn intellectual and moral authority over to him. I also am accepting his affection as my due. I deserve it since it comes from him. His affection has transformed me into a lovable person.

"No one ever called me Sunshine," I say. He sends me a photograph of a giant pile of cut logs. He is not in the picture. He sounds measured and assertive, a man who is comfortable in his own skin.

One day he asks me if I am single. He has already

asked me this same question. Is he running out of material? A wave of clarity washes over me. It occurrs to me that he must be writing to another woman, or even to several others. I return to his Facebook profile, and photographs of two women flash up on the screen. One is tall and thin with long dark hair. Her picture is much larger and more prominent.

So, I conclude that he is hedging his bets, cultivating two or more women, as many catfish do. This time, I ask Devlin outright. *Are you writing to other women?* But as innocent and straightforward as Devlin has seemed, he knows exactly what to do. He ignores my question, as if I had never exposed his *faux pas*. He never makes this mistake again.

Some of the lessons from *Catfish: The TV show*, are obvious even if they don't apply to me. You should have hard evidence that someone is who they say they are. You should never trust anyone whom you've never met. Of course, how could I meet Devlin since he is in Cuba? These truisms may be more obvious to the MTV crowd than to women the age of their mothers and grandmothers who came of age in a world balanced between honest men and outright scoundrels whom you should never, under any circumstances, trust.

On Sunday he asks, "How are you spending the day, Joan?" My first impulse is to tell the truth. It is rare for him to use my given name. My next impulse is to decline (as Fidel Castro famously once said in a far more serious context, *"para qué?"*).

I wonder whether my having written many books will frighten away this logger who never went to college. Still, perhaps this may have been the case when I was young but is no longer so. Wasn't one of the victories of the 1970s that men now appreciated accomplished, even intellectual, women?

Devlin never notices that I have written about Haiti or that I was interviewed for a film. Still, I am uneasy. I had been married for a decade to a man who read every word I wrote, sometimes even making suggestions in an elegant cursive handwriting.

It does not occur to me to lie. Lying, as Marlow famously says in Joseph Conrad's *Heart of Darkness*, bears the "taint of mortality." I have believed this to be true all my life, and not even the virtual caresses of Devlin could change that.

This was now a two-tier romance where I found myself having been thrust backward in history. We were less civilized now than in the world where we pushed toward equality between men and women.

Apropos of nothing, Devlin tells me that I am beautiful. This amazes me because I know it isn't true. The only man who believed I was beautiful was the aforementioned husband and he was not a conventional person, to say the least. He defined himself, as did Leon Trotsky, as a "revolutionary."

Among my father's last words to me were, "You were never pretty," which was devastating with a sting that has never left me. Now, however, I have Devlin's revision. Even if he has only a Facebook photograph, clearly marked with a date, 2009, he has decided that I am "beautiful."

He wishes me a blessed Sunday. "Oh, you're religious," I say.

"Well, I would consider myself religious and a little bit spiritual too," Devlin replies. "I was raised Catholic. My mom was a great astrologer, very beautiful, very vain, very smart, and kind. She read Tarot cards, and she could tell if good fortune is coming your way by just reading your palm. As time went on, she stopped believing in Horoscope and gave her life to Christ before she passed on."

This went straight to my heart. He was real and authentic, sweet, and lovable. I have to admit, my friends who grew up in Catholic homes have exhibited higher moral characters, greater generosity of spirit and unselfishness.. They were all women, however.

In a parody of our being new lovers, we share our histories. I tell him that I grew up in the Bronx where you didn't see many trees, where trees were alien presences, rare and inaccessible. This inspires Devlin to tell me about his childhood and his father.

It is just June 14th. "Was working with my dad at a very young age cutting trees for Custer Sawmill, and I fell in love with logging. My Dad was my hero, he was such a sweet guy, he was probably too sweet, very successful in the logging business. He made a lot of money. He was one of the second generation of loggers. Too bad both my parents are gone now. I really miss them so much."

This is sweet and touching. Surely it is evidence that he is a good person, one worthy of being loved.

June 15, PM: "Hi Joan, just finished working here about an hour ago. Relaxing and enjoying some bbq ribs and salad for dinner … wanna come and join me? Lol."

Who could blame me for replying, "Yes, I would love to join you where you are." I still had no idea where he was. No scent of Cuba had surfaced in his many emails, no names of Cuban artists or musicians.

On June 16th, at 10:42 in the morning Devlin writes: "Trust me, Joan. I believe there is a lot of time we can get to know more about ourselves and see where it goes from there. I believe that imagination is stronger than knowledge. That myth is more potent than history. Dreams are more powerful than facts. That hope always triumphs over experience. That laughter is the only cure for grief. And I believe that love is stronger than death."

His tone has changed. This does not sound like the Devlin I have come to know. Some of it sounds like a Jimmy Buffett song written near the end of his life. Nor do I subscribe to most of it. I believe that history is more powerful than myth, although right-wing politicians, terrified of history, might tell you otherwise. I also believe that dreams *are* facts. I wish it were true, but alas, I don't believe that love is stronger than death. I will never get over the death of the husband mentioned earlier.

I would also insist that knowledge lays down a path to survival. I am skeptical of this Devlin. I am also suspicious of the flattery in which Devlin has begun to indulge. "Good morning, Joan," he had written only two hours before he sent forth his credo. "Neither a cup of coffee nor sweet chocolate can make me feel better. All I need to make a great start of my day is to think about you."

25

I try to persuade him that I am not the person he seems to believe that I am. "You might have gathered that I am tough and straightforward," I say. "To get an idea, you have to read one of my books. You might not like that person so much."

"You really seem to be a nice woman, Joan," he answers, ignoring the warning. "And yes, I'm really looking forward to meeting you someday. I'll be very glad." Now he offers some personal history:

"Ever since I got divorced, I've been in two different relationships, but it doesn't turn out great for me. The first lady was disrespectful. She has begged me to come back on emails. I said no. You got too comfortable with me, and I allowed it. Get over it."

I believe, very emphatically, that we never get over anything, so I felt a pang here. I said nothing about my own views to him. A lesson I learned long ago is that you should feel no obligation to tell all that you know - to anyone.

"Everything she said about me is true, however she lacks social skills. She wouldn't say those things to anyone else. My last relationship was toxic whereby she lied of her bed partner to be her brother not until I had gotten to know they were both cheating on me. I was emotionally down during that time but I'm over it."

I am at a loss. What should I say? I fear that my answer offered little solace, "Maybe two people have to be looking for the same thing," I say, "at the same time, and be beyond criticizing and trying to change the other person." I don't know what I'm talking about. I have too little to go on. I ignore his very bad English.

He goes silent and I fear that I have ruined everything. I wait until ten at night and then I write, "Michael, if I said something that offended you, please allow me to apologize." The locution comes of course from the Rolling Stones song "Sympathy for the Devil," where Lucifer begins as if he were a civilized human being, "Please allow me to introduce myself…"

I must wait. I wait. There is no way to clarify any of this, no way to fill in the narrative. Finally, Devlin answers, only to again try to persuade me to switch over to Google Chat. I tell him that a former student is coming over on Tuesday and perhaps she knows what Google Chat is and can get me on to it.

Now he shows an interest in my books. "Just keep me posted whenever your books are available."

"When you're back, I will send some to you." So far, I have told myself that I believed every word he has said. His English is faulty. Otherwise, I do not detect a scam.

"One fun fact about me," he volunteers, "I'm a firm believer that things only have as much power as you give them. I want to focus on being a good partner, a supportive friend and simply enjoy my days in a way that feels natural."

I tell him he is already a supportive friend, and for no reason I mention an old friend of mine, now deceased, named Martin F. Dardis. Marty had been a police investigator in Miami attached to the office of the district attorney. He had never progressed beyond the third grade and for the rest of his life felt compelled to prove himself the sharpest investigator, the smartest man in the room and the sexiest too, although he was short and fat and had a wide bulbous nose.

Having enlisted in World War Two, Marty found himself at the Battle of the Bulge where he killed many German soldiers and contracted a case of frostbite that would plague him for the rest of his life. Night or day, he was always searching for a pair of socks. Once he picked up a pair of my navy silk socks from the bathroom floor and just put them on without a word. This didn't prevent him from breaking the Watergate case.

Marty stepped back. Credit was never what he was seeking. Bob Woodward and Carl Bernstein at once wrapped themselves in the glory.

Realizing he had made a mistake, Marty considered suing Woodward and Bernstein, over the film *All The President's Men*, then decided against it. It was not his style to ask for anything for himself. He preferred the honesty of James McCord.

I share with Devlin that Marty had been the chief crime researcher at *Sports Illustrated* magazine. That his name didn't appear on his *SI* research didn't bother him at all. Those he respected knew of his accomplishments and that was enough.

Marty delighted in irony. He enjoyed having arrested the television personality, Larry King, twice, always with forensic evidence in hand. He could always make me laugh. Picking up a no-account witness at the Miami Airport, he held up a sign, "Mr. Wonderful." Forced to retrieve a somewhat paranoid individual on a night when Marty had Dolphins tickets, he was told by his witness that the Black people collecting the airport trash were spies for J. Edgar Hoover. Marty rejoined, "No, they're emptying Hoover's wastebaskets."

In his last year, Marty filled out the paperwork so that he could be buried at Arlington National Cemetery – among his life ambitions. To the end, he remained proud of his Silver Star, an award that in those days was primarily reserved for the dead. Marty's last words to me were, "NEVER TRUST ANYONE," spoken emphatically in his deep, husky voice. He did not expect a reply from me, and of course I had none.

On the *Catfish* show, a victim named Brittany pleads, "Who can I trust?" The host, Kamie, who has taken the place of the no-nonsense Max, my favorite, bursts out, "NO ONE!" This was the world of Dardis discourse too.

* * *

"The lying makes me less attracted to you," one victim tells his catfish. The world presided over by the Internet is not worth inhabiting for those who know better.

Devlin ventures an actual question. "You are in New Jersey, right?"

I challenged him to guess which baseball team I root for.

"I'm guessing you probably cheer for the Jackals," he replies. Who? His email is accompanied by an emoji of an animal, maybe a fox or a jackal. As a sports fan, and a baseball fan since I was four or five years old, with Yankee Stadium in walking distance, I know there is no such major league team, not in the American or in the National League.

Devlin tells me he has taken a photograph of himself working "this morning." There he is in a brilliant color picture, a handsome grey-haired man seated behind the wheel of a gigantic glass-fronted machine in the middle of a thick forest. It is a middle shot of a man in very tight jeans. You can still make out his smiling face, a face that exudes joy.

Effortlessly, he manages the gigantic machine. He seems beautiful. His boots sit quietly behind his chair. His feet are encased in rainbow socks, white with a band of colors, mainly purple, around the ankles. His legs are long and lean, so he is probably tall. He has a sweet smile, grey hair, and a grey goatee, as he had in his Facebook photographs. His hands are large, and I want to touch them. I yearn for his hands to touch me.

I remember the eminent fiction writer, Robert Olen Butler, visiting the writing program at Temple University one winter and telling my students that all stories are about love and that love is defined by "yearning." We didn't get the point. We were all puzzled. Graduate students all, they were too young, and I, I must admit, too old. So this was what Bob meant! It has taken me years to figure it out.

In his logging machine photograph Devlin seems contented, a person without malice. Just by looking at his picture you can tell he is a good man at work at his chosen profession. "Did you receive the photograph," he asks without guile. "I took it this morning."

I cannot admit to him that I am mesmerized by this photograph. I look at it obsessively until it sinks into the quagmire of my emails. I ask him to send it to me again. He complies.

I check whether there is any trace of Cuba in that picture. There is not, as far as I can tell, but I do not trust myself on this question. I tell him again that I have written a book about Cuba, but in his next message he makes no reference to it.

He asks no questions. He supplies no information. Where in Cuba is he working? What are his impressions of post-Castro Cuba? For whom is he working and what is his assignment in Cuba? He leaves the length of his stay indefinite.

The following Saturday morning he confides that he is doing laundry. It is pleasant that he is drawing me into his domestic life. *We are together.* "I love my job so much," he writes.

He tells me that he loves to travel and talks about all the places he has been. When I tell him that I have spent time in Japan, his response is unthreatened. He assumes, wrongly, that I went to Japan as a tourist. He cannot imagine my life as a writer. In fact, I went to Japan for the first time on a work trip. Here is how that came about. A digression:

It was in 1972. I was married to revolutionary social activist Ralph Schoenman. We were living near Princeton, New Jersey where he had gone to school. I was a film historian doing research on the Algerian War for independence from France at the Near East library of Princeton University when Ralph spied a notice on one of the bulletin boards. It was titled "Japan and the Japanese." The *Mainichi Shimbun* news-

Ralph Schoenman

papers were sponsoring an essay contest, open to people in any country, on the theme of how they viewed Japan and Japanese culture and identity.

Swiftly, almost as if he had not so much as moved a muscle, Ralph took down the announcement and put it in his pocket. I was shocked. Wasn't that illegal? In those days, I held Princeton

University in reverence; having attended a vastly inferior college – I knew my place.

Ralph, who in his years at Princeton had fought Cold War battles with the administration, did not worship Princeton, no matter its top ranking in the country. Ralph had hosted as

Sherlock visiting the offices of the *Mainichi Shimbun* newspapers, Tokyo, 1972.

speakers before the students Howard Fast and Alger Hiss, not without opposition from Dean Bill Lippincott, dean of students. (Later Lippincott would be exposed as CIA's representative at Princeton.) By now, Ralph had nothing to fear from Princeton. in keeping with CIA's own practice, the definite article is omitted. "THE CIA is a locution reserved for outsiders."

So within a week, two essays I had written about Japanese film director Akira Kurosawa were on their way to Japan and the contest. A few months later, Ralph was on the telephone with a new friend, a *Mainichi* stringer posted to the U.S. named Hirome Seki. He had called with the news that I was among ten winners world-wide, the only one from the United States.

"I'm not going," I said.

My successes meant more to Ralph than his own. He pressured me to attend a lecture at the Japan Society in New York to hear Donald Richie, the foremost English language historian of Japanese cinema. I went to Japan and made an appointment to meet with Richie, a meeting that almost didn't happen because Richie affected to be lost between the old and the new wings of the Imperial Hotel. Located in central Tokyo, this was so notorious a hangout that it was inconceivable to both me and my host, Mr. Kyushiro Kusakabe, that Richie could not find his way around there.

In the coming years, I went on to write five books about Japan and Japanese film. In my novel, *Natural Tendencies*," Richie appears as among the most intriguing characters. Richie himself professed to like the book.

Too much to explain to an Internet suitor.

"I'm impressed!" Devlin replied to the news that I had been to Japan. "Never been to Japan once, but I would love to someday. Have already lived in St. Quentin, France when I was young before moving to the States. I have been out of the States several times on different occasions, on a work trip or vacation trip. My work has taken me to places like Canada, Sweden, and other parts of the States. On vacation trips with my daughter, I have been to Mexico, Germany, Switzerland, Milan, Italy (my last trip since 2019), Yugoslavia, Greece, Bermuda, Paris, Rio de Janeiro of Brazil, and Dubai." The list is so long that it takes up four inches of screen space.

"I would love my next vacation trip to be with that special someone," he adds, "because I don't believe I'm destined to travel this road alone. I look forward to sharing my last journey in love, laughter & friendship." I sense that he is attempting to appeal to what he surmises are my needs, but I can't be certain.

"Loving a woman is no longer enough for me," Devlin writes. "The genuine friendship that develops, enjoying each other's company, the ability to communicate one's needs, desires, hopes & dreams, for me, will sustain the relationship."

He has invoked the term "love," a concept that has been devalued by an epidemic of scams. I force myself to ignore clichés like "special someone." I blanche when I hear a catfish victim on MTV say, "I just want someone to love me."

The list of Devlin's travels seemed hyperbolic, but I believed him. In two separate emails, he repeats the story of his two most recent relationships. This came unsolicited. It seems as if he is following a checklist.

The more serious of the two began online, by email. She had not respected me, he says. "She had been right about what she said about me," he says, but he still did not want to be in contact with her again. The word "respect" appears again. She kept on emailing, but he did not reply.

Woman number two's story arrived this time in a jumble. Apparently he had caught her with another man whom she claimed was her brother, only for that not to have been the case. I did not pry. I did not ask that he elaborate. Truth be told,

I did not want to know. Either I didn't want to awaken my jealous nature, or I did not want to diminish him in my eyes. No doubt it was both. It occurs to me again that he is running out of material. He has told me about these two "relationships" twice.

On June 17th, at 10:00 at night, he writes, "Well, to be honest, let me just say both of the ladies I dated in the past were so wishy-washy ... I must say that honesty and loyalty seem to be lacking in today's relationships, even marriages, and it's so sad. I'm honest to a fault, so I'm up front with all the bits."

"You seem like such a terrific guy," I write. "I can't figure out why those women you told me about didn't please you more. Or make it work." Then I go on to address the "wishy-washy" point. Here, I believe, I am on high ground. No one has ever accused me of being weak-minded, of not having strong views.

"Well, I am as far from wishy-washy as could be," I say. "But don't take my word for it. My books are very strong, even defiant, and focus on controversial subjects. One is called *A Farewell to Justice*. The subject is the JFK assassination. *Blood in the Water* is about the attack on the USS *Liberty*, an intelligence ship, in 1967. It is a work of history.

"Maybe you already know all this," I backtrack. Then, to soften the moment, I add, "I also know what it means to be uncompromisingly honest. There's a price you pay for that."

I seem to be bragging shamelessly. He is bringing out the worst in me, I realize, another "red flag," as they say on *Catfish*, portending rough waters. I am disgusted with myself for begging him to read my books. Maybe it is because he is not real to me. Devlin is no stranger to excuses, whereas I have adopted the mantra of one of my favorite characters, the Texan Robert J. Kleberg, Jr., who ran the most magnificent ranch in the United States, the King Ranch: "No excuses!" was Kleberg's motto. Kleberg was the real-life main character in George Stevens' epic film *Giant*. It was great fun writing about him in my book, *The Great Game in Cuba*.

Along with the joys of being a non-fiction writer and a biographer, I suffered many dark experiences. One involved the forensic pathologist from Pittsburgh Cyril Wecht. My biographical subject, Jim Garrison, had gone into federal court in Washington D.C. to obtain autopsy photographs of President Kennedy. He was opposed by the Kennedy family. Cyril Wecht, who knew the evidence, and had doubts about Oswald's guilt, had followed the Garrison case. Yet Wecht refused to testify for Garrison. Later he would make a career of his expertise on the Kennedy assassination. *When it counted, he had not been available.*

* * *

In Louisiana, there was an entity devoted to thwarting implementation of Brown v. Board of Education (1954), the Supreme Court case that outlawed segregation. An investigator for the Sovereignty Commission named Anne Dischler went to work for Garrison. Dischler was very shrewd and hardworking; Garrison did not hire people based on their politics, and that she opposed integration of the public schools did not disqualify her from working for him. Her own children had been home-schooled. That Dischler had shared her handwritten notebooks with another writer was enough for me to contact her for an appointment.

Very early one morning I drove my rental car onto the raft from St. Francisville to New Roads and then kept driving deep into Louisiana. This road would take me to Texas had that been my destination. I was early and sat in Anne Dischler's yard for an hour. Finally, it seemed as if time had gone south. I got out of the car.

I went around to the trunk to extract the weathered red velvet briefcase that contained my tape machine and writing pads – I would use both – only to look up and find Mrs. Dischler standing in front of me. She was a wiry, late middle-aged woman who had obviously once been a great beauty.

"Don't do that!" she said harshly. She had changed her mind about talking to me and I must get off her property. Tears sprang to my eyes. I made the standard arguments ... including that Patricia Lambert had revealed herself to be working for an intelligence service. It took another year of begging and pleading for me to gain access to Mrs. Dischler's notebooks. But I did.

There were many high moments too. On that same day, as I drove back to the ferry landing, I was racing to keep an appointment with Corrie Collins, who had been Chairman of CORE (the Congress of Racial Equality) and who had witnessed Lee Harvey Oswald in the company of David Ferrie and Clay Shaw. No matter how many times I telephoned, I reached an answering machine. Collins had been undergoing dialysis several times a week. Perhaps it was too late.

I called Garrison's chief assistant, John Volz. "Just go up and knock on the door," Volz said. I felt like a fool, a child, an inexperienced woman.

So I drove to the Collins' house and knocked. The screen door, torn in several places, was open. Corrie Collins stood just inside. His father stood behind him. You couldn't do an honest book about Oswald in Louisiana without talking to Corrie Collins.

The other crucial interview was with an avowed enemy of Corrie Collins named John R. Rarick, who was the sitting district judge in the Feliciana parishes. My friend, writer Anne Butler, who operated an exquisite bed and breakfast on her family plantation, was a rare liberal Democrat in that part of Louisiana. She told me that

Oswald

Ferrie

Shaw

when she ran into Judge Rarick in St. Francisville she would cross the street to avoid him. He had a David Duke campaign card under the glass top of his old-fashioned wooden desk. My heart leapt into my throat when I saw it, but I kept my mouth shut.

Judge Rarick did his first interview with me wearing Bermuda shorts, but I couldn't have written my book without him. One Sunday, he even did an interview *for* me with John Manchester, the town marshal, who had a confrontation in Clinton, Louisiana with Garrison suspect Clay Shaw.

The two, Rarick and Manchester, attended the same church. Rarick, a sincere racist who threw black people out of his courtroom for wearing a T-shirt, was helping this white radical NY Jewish intellectual supporter of the civil rights movement to *find out who killed President Kennedy* – plus I was writing a book about his law school classmate Jim Garrison. Even so, after church Judge Rarick asked John Manchester a set of questions provided to him by me!

There was no clear and obvious path to the reality of the events surrounding the Kennedy assassination. Arriving in Dallas nursing a broken tooth, I met the great lady of assassination research, Mary Ferrell. Without many preliminaries, Mary handed me the heavy unpublished manuscript written by Tom Bethel, a plant in Garrison's office. It was a detailed play-by-play of Bethel's efforts to scuttle the Garrison case.

Mary Ferrell surveying her archive

It included an angry encounter with John Manchester.

Mary directed me to a little hotel a block away where I could use the Xerox machine. My apprenticeship was progressing.

At the end of seven years, I emerged as at least friendly with both Rarick and Dischler. It turned out that Rarick's loyalty was to the truth, as he revealed in another of my investigations, that into the 1967 bombing of the USS *Liberty*. He was a Congressman then, and I came upon his speech on the House floor in the Congressional Record. Rare among government officials, Rarick demanded a full investigation of what happened to the USS *Liberty*. He was ignored.

Would Devlin have been interested in my research in the state where he claimed to have grown up? I did not share any of these adventures with him.

* * *

It's still only June 17th. It appears that we have all the time in the world to get to know each other, although the quote from my biography of Lillian Hellman and Dashiell Hammett comes to mind again.

With Devlin, I am content to remain in the realm of small talk. "What is your favorite dinner?" I want to know. Having been born in France, he must know something about food. His reply is disappointing: "I'd say prime ribs, pasta, chicken quesadillas and meatloaf." He said he grew up in Louisiana, but no word about crawfish étouffée, gumbo, even a hint of seafood, the oysters so luxuriant in that state. Then comes a remark whose veracity I doubt: "I love to cook but haven't been cooking much lately, it's hard to cook for one."

"What about you, Joan?"

I like good Chinese food, I say. I am thinking of my friend, the author and filmmaker John Nathan, the Japanese expert who deplored the fast-food Chinese restaurants seemingly unavoidable in Tokyo. I tell Devlin that I love to swim, and that I have a pool, and that I love the ocean, although this may be too much information. He may conclude that I am rich, and hence an easy and appropriate target.

The problem is that we have nothing in common. I talk about the theatre in New York, and the play I had most recently seen, "Leopoldtstadt," which wasn't very good. As Tom Stoppard's supposed effort to address his hitherto unacknowledged Jewish ancestry, this was a subject I was debating with my friend Caroline Seebohm, with whom I attended many Stoppard plays over the years only for her to meet an untimely death in 2023. As he has ignored the references to my books, so now Devlin does not address the issue of Stoppard's Jewish heritage. I wonder if he has ever been to New York. It occurs to me that he has not. I doubt if he has ever met, let alone befriended, a Jewish person....

"I like basketball games," I add, "and once wrote a book about it; I had a great teacher on that." He evades this subject too and doesn't ask me the name of that great teacher, depriving me of the opportunity of mentioning Coach Bob Knight. It could be that he never heard of Bob Knight just as he never heard of the playwright Tom Stoppard.

Who is this man?

"OK, that is nice," Devlin finally says with no apparent intellectual curiosity. Then he moves on to the safe ground of the weather. "The weather here is delightful," he says, "sunny, warm. Did laundry this morning and just relaxing now… basically nothing much to do here." He exhibits no interest in Cuba. "Me, my co-workers, we live in a Bunk House. So tell me, Joan, what do you do for fun on your leisure times?"

Of course, I cannot tell him the truth, that I have no leisure times, holidays, or weekends. "When I am writing a book," I say, "There are no holidays." Perhaps only a fellow writer would understand this. I tell him that I am writing a book that I plan to call "Dear Sherlock."

Has he ever heard of Sherlock Holmes?

"Will you do something for me, Sunshine?" he writes. "Will you just picture your life for me five years from now, and ten years from now? What's it look like?"

I choose the five-year figure. I am not comfortable with imagining myself being alive in ten years. It occurs to me that Devlin may believe that I am younger than I am. These are the kind of questions men ask women in Hallmark TV specials. They are not questions I would ever ask myself.

* * *

I have never been brave or imaginative enough to look ahead, which is why I chose to major in English, a flat outworn field of study.

The obvious choice for me was physical anthropology. So, my kind instructor tried to encourage me on the last day of class as he was about to move on from Hunter College, in the Bronx, a form of high school extension, a stopping off place for scholars on their way to better places. He had been hired by the archaeology department at the University of Arizona.

Mr. Hartle told me I was the best in the class. I was especially skilled at identifying the body parts of a variety of species. The deep past beckoned me.

I was so shy that I stood there, mute. Then I walked away, never to see or communicate with David Hartle again. I remember that I was wearing a mustard-colored jersey dress with a wide brown woven belt. The dress was ripped inside, but you couldn't see that. I was ashamed, nonetheless. All these decades later, I remember that brief encounter vividly.

* * *

Five years' time seems more manageable. I try to conjure up literary ambitions, but truth be told I had none. I considered my investigatory efforts, but no crimes that I might pursue came to mind. I had no interest in material possessions or in real estate. I love my secluded country house.

Would I be alone, like now? But this is not a subject to be shared with a man whose voice I have never heard.

I outline the five-year scenario. I imagine myself and Devlin in a little cottage by the sea. He sketches himself into the scene sitting by my side. Neither of us allow the intrusion of global warming which renders my fantasy obsolete, an anachronism. If such a mirage had ever been possible, it is barely imaginable now in a world of mud and falling, rushing waters, and floods.

He replies that I am "sweet." Leaving aside the five- and ten-year scenarios, Devlin returns to more stable concerns. "Good thing we are not working today," he writes. "So enough time for me to rest and do some laundry. How are you doing today, Sweetheart?"

So I have graduated from "Sunshine" to the more intimate "Sweetheart."

Later Devlin evokes my dream of a cottage by the water. "What would I be doing, staring at you?" he asks in a rare moment of irritation. I drop the subject. Neither of us ever mentions it again. His credo has been never to disagree with me about anything, never to criticize me. This fact alone may be viewed as a red flag, penetrating a fraudulent scenario.

The "correct" answer to the inane question of what you will be doing in either five- or ten-years' time, as Hallmark TV would have it, is that you will be married and cuddling a newborn. This was never my ambition, not even when I was nineteen and first married.

I tell him that I am a solitary person. Unprovoked, he confides that he just checked on Facebook, "and it shows we are still friends." I think, this is odd, why would he think that I have blocked him as a friend, a practice apparently habitual on Facebook? What has led him to believe that I am suspicious of him?

"Good morning, Joan," he writes at 2:23 in the afternoon; I have no idea what time of the day it is in Cuba. He writes again that he believes we should move our communication from emails to Google Chat.

"All you have to do is just sign in and that's all," he says, "I know it may be difficult for the first time, but once you get through it, then it's good to go."

I do not trust his insistence that I move to a different computer system, although I do not say that.

IV

GOOD DAY SUNSHINE!

He is still calling me "Sunshine." He presents himself as keeping to a rigorous schedule: 6:00 AM off to work, off between 5:00 and 6:00, writing to me between 7:00 and 8:00 PM. He has made himself seem available. There is no room for anyone else. He never mentions the daughter with whom he took so many exotic trips.

As a woman of a certain age, I fear that Devlin will be disappointed, an apprehension I share with Gabriel García Márquez's characters in *Love in The Time of Cholera*, people who find physical and spiritual love only near the end of their lives. For Gabo, there is no distinction between the various moments of love. At first, Fermina Daza insists that she and Florentino Ariza make love only with the lights out.

Sherlock interviewing Colombian Nobel Prize Winning novelist Gabriel García Márquez in Mexico City, 1984.

I broach this subject carefully. "There are a few things I need to tell you," I begin. "No, I am not dying of cancer or a heart ailment. I thought you were a person to whom impediments didn't matter."

"Trust me, Sunshine," Devlin says gently. "I know this may sound bizarre to you, but do you have any idea how much I like you? I had no intention of falling for you, but you made me love again. You've brought back those hopes and dreams to my life once again. A few months ago, I was thinking of how to start a new job after my retirement and my usual daily routine life, but all I can think now is looking forward to the future with you in it." He closes with an emoji, a quizzical expression plastered across its face.

"Falling for you" is a common catfish locution. At one point on the MTV series, Nev reports that the term "catfish" has now appeared in the Merriam Webster dictionary. There are also new locutions related to on-line dating. "To DM" means to "direct message." These initials, DM, now function as a verb.

The practice of catfishing has proliferated. There is no law against it as there is no punishment for lying in general. On the TV program the 24-year-old co-host Kamie tells an especially egregious offender, "There is such a thing as morality."

"I don't know what that means," the catfish, whose name is Tony, answers, unimpressed. Caught out, you lie. There are no consequences. A catfish admits to Nev that he could never think of a victim of one of his scams in a romantic way.

Devlin grows more affectionate. On June 19th, he writes: "I wish you could see the difference you make in my life since we started talking. I run to my phone each day just to read from you." At such moments I wonder again whether he is a native English speaker.

"It is my wish at this point in time," he says, "to really find a good woman with a good mind. A woman that is caring and knows what it takes to really stand for his [sic] man no matter the situation and as I am also willing to stand no matter what." I think of Ralph's travails in both England and the US, not least with the *New York Times*.

"And this is the simple reason why I had to continue this communication with you," Devlin goes on, "as I do not regret it at all as you are the type of woman that I deserve and hunger for." I believe every word of this. I am convinced of his sincerity. "I must tell you," he says, "that I am so happy to hear from you and also for your simplicity for having me as a friend."

"I feel the same way," I say. "It makes me very happy to hear from you. I think we're more than friends, although not everything requires a name." I bring myself to add: "I also note that you don't ask me too many questions. The truth will come out," as one of my subjects once said, referring to the Kennedy assassination, although that statement applies to many situations.

I am referring to Jim Garrison. Garrison was replying to a distressed former New Orleans homicide detective, L.J. Delsa, who came to Garrison upset by the obfuscations of the House Select Committee investigating the Kennedy assassination in the late 1970s. It was apparent to most that the Warren Commission had failed in its mandate to uncover who had organized Kennedy's murder. Now the government was trying again.

"The truth will come out," Garrison said dryly.

I am reasonably certain that Michael Devlin has never heard of Jim Garrison. I do not mention Garrison's name to him.

When Devlin tells me that he admires a woman who has a strong work ethic, I decide that we are perfectly suited to each other. By now, I have had 24 books published. I have also spent a lot of time on my students' manuscripts, covering in many cases a full yellow pad with comments, not always to the student's pleasure.

I tell Devlin that I don't compete with the men in my life. And that I admire humility, not to be confused with weakness.

"I would like the telephone," I say, including an emoji of a black telephone receiver in the old style, "but we can wait. How can it be that although we've never spoken, I miss you?"

Devlin has a ready reply. "I believe that we know enough about each other, which is not too much, but enough to say we are not complete strangers. I see that you are a very good woman, sweet, intelligent, and respectful. You may meet a person and instantly know that you will be best friends forever. Other friendships develop over an extended period of time. In some friendships you may feel a sense of equality, while in others there may be a clear sense that one is giving more to the friendship than the other. There are no rules about how a friendship has to be."

I don't believe that we can assign some tonalities, some locutions, to women and others to men. Yet it occurs to me that these sentences read as if they were written by a woman.

The voice then returns to one I would expect of Devlin. "If you are able to share your life with another human being," he (or she) writes, "By all means, go right ahead. All friendships are unique and special in their own way. Each one is valuable."

Yes, we have returned to the realm of cliché. It seems clear again that Devlin is not an intellectual, that he swims in different waters. Yet certainly, I tell myself, he is not to be written off. Among the most romantic films I have ever seen was directed by Italian director Lina Wertmuller. We appeared together on the Bill Boggs television program on channel 5 in New York in the days when ideas were still being debated on daytime television. The film was called *Swept Away By An Unusual Destiny In The Blue Sea of August*. An upper-class woman is stranded on an uninhabited island in the Mediterranean with a working-class sailor. In that film, class trumps love, and at the end the lovers are separated forever. In real life, however, surely it need not be so. Devlin's lack of education need not be so complete an obstacle to our finding that seaside scene of bliss.

"So has Audrey figured out how to install Google Chat on your device yet?" he writes. I admit that people in her office use Google Chat."Yup, I told you so, lol," he replies. When that very morning, AOL crashes, I ask him, "Are you the kind who says, 'I told you so'?"

He laughs.

It is June 19th, just eight days since we first "talked": Devlin suddenly softens. "It's always nice to read from you," he writes. "There's this eagerness I feel inside of me to get more closer to you. You're very easy to talk to and I feel I could tell you anything. It's nice to step back and be able to see the big picture in life. What are the qualities you seek in a man?"

"Generosity of spirit, supportiveness if that's a word, male energy which has nothing to do with what someone looks like. Loyalty in all its many meanings," I answer.

One morning Devlin falls ill with a respiratory ailment He never misses work, he says. But today he cannot get out of bed. As if he were part of my life, as if I knew him, it grieves me that he is in distress. I long to help take care of him. "I was so weak," he writes. "That's why I couldn't text you the whole of yesterday." I long to put my arms around him, to soothe his pain.

"When the medical staff came to check on me," he writes, "they said it was the flu." He adds a sorrowful emoji. Then he continues his habitual discourse. "PS: I really missed talking to you yesterday. I hope you had a wonderful day, Joan, and a blissful weekend."

"A relief to hear from you," I say. "I hope you feel better today. Sorry to pry, but did they give you a COVID test? Maybe the term "common cold" rules out COVID?" I had been terrified when, in the early days of the pandemic, it seemed virtually impossible to obtain the vaccine in the state of New Jersey. Finally, I telephoned the office of my congresswoman. Her response was to send two police officers to my door. They refused to come inside, although I invited them to do so.

A week later, out of the blue, I received a telephone call from someone in the township health department. Could I come to the local elementary school for my first shot? I could and I did.

"Yeah," he says, "and I was tested Negative." He does not have COVID. "They said I had a flu." That was fast, I thought, another doubt that I push aside. All I say, however, is, "Full disclosure: I missed hearing from you today."

"Currently laying down on my bed with a blanket on," he says. "I'm feeling a little more better today," he says. "How are you doing today?"

I am relieved as if relief were a physically palpable object. I feel as if his physical well-being were of great interest to me. I love him. The next day he says that his crew has insisted that he remain in bed. Another day passes and he is back on the job.

* * *

In the early morning of June 20th, he is more talkative.

"Good morning, Sunshine," he writes. "Feeling a lot better today. My crewmen said I should rest the whole day, 'don't worry, pal, we got this under control'. So definitely I'm gonna start working by tomorrow. I was already sleeping when you texted yesterday. What you said really resonated with me. I like physical affection as well. I show PDA and also don't mind kissing in public."

I have no idea what PDA means. Audrey knows. It means "Public Displays of Affection." I am charmed. Does it mean that he wants to put his arms around me? Does it mean that he wants to hold hands in front of other people? Does it mean that he would kiss me in front of other people? I remember being horrified when standing in a movie line and my husband put his arms around me, and I shook him off. I am no longer that person. Was I getting a second chance?

"Another fact about me is that I'm a very romantic man and a good kisser too (think I have a gold medal for that)." This is followed by two emoji lips, three medals hanging from ribbons, and four emoji faces with various expressions and moods. It does not occur to me that I may not ever cash in on all those promised kisses. Vaguely, I imagine kissing him.

I am increasingly nervous about the prospect of meeting him. The moment seems to be drawing closer. During these last days of June, he is reassuring as he reiterates that he is looking forward to our meeting.

Again, I wonder whether he is a native English speaker. The issue dances through my mind only to dissolve in the heat of my enthusiasm for him.

More platitudes follow. "I like a woman [with] loyalty, honesty, good work ethic, caring, trustworthy, good sense of humour [yes, I note the British spelling], intelligence, confident (but not cocky) and thoughtful," he writes. It all sounds as if it comes out of a book, one published in Great Britain. I am mildly alarmed. I am distracted by all the inconsistencies.

Devlin now responds to my efforts to lure him into reading my books. He does not acquiesce, however. "Life is short and precious," he writes. "I don't want to waste time basing my life and relationships on things that don't really matter in the long run." That books "don't matter in the long run" is as distant from my point of view as you can get.

Should I have ghosted Devlin at this point? Audrey taught me about ghosting – without a warning you just disappear from the other person's life. Instead, I attempt again to explain myself. I tell him too much. "I am not talented at forgiveness," I say. There are two recordings now playing in my brain. One hopes that every word he has said is true, that the qualities he wanted in a woman were also qualities he shared. I tell him I prefer "just plain goodness, which means you would not be sympathetic to a Donald Trump." I add: "You have never said anything political." The other tape doubts his every utterance, doubts that he is even in Cuba, doubts that he is an American or even a native English speaker.

He does not take the bait. I tell him that I am a strong supporter of the First Amendment. Does he even know what the First Amendment is?

He does not respond to the mentions of Trump. "Were you censoring yourself when you saw the words "Kennedy Assassination?" I inquire.

His lack of response may not be surprising to the reader, but even if he was behaving in his habitual manner, it felt to me that the mention of Trump should have inspired a response. It is now late at night. Perhaps at this hour he simply cannot bring himself to talk about this horrific event, the Kennedy assassination. Still, I cannot ignore the fact that he did not react as I would have expected him to have done. Obviously, the murder of this president means nothing to him.

But I am not ready to give up on Devlin. I offer a puerile response to his lack of interest in my work. "I think you're saying that what's in my books doesn't really tell us anything. Maybe you're right. Many of my friends haven't read them. The people who write to me on Facebook are invariably the ones who have. You may be thinking, so what!"

Full disclosure to my perhaps horrified reader: one of the aforementioned Catholic women friends of mine had not read the Haiti book which I gave her, and that hurt me. At a pre-Christmas lunch, when I realized that she had no interest in my books, I felt my heart turn to ice. Her surname was Moriarity, and she shared her Irishness with everyone named Devlin. I continued to long to send him one of my books since I believe that they are me at my best. I would have to wait until I summoned the nerve to ask him for his address. I still had no telephone number either. I didn't know the name of the company for which he was working, I didn't know the Cuban city where he was based.

V

LOVERS?

We lurch forward. His tone changes as if he has somehow reached another level of passion. He has unveiled a new metaphor. He claims he has dropped into a deep canyon from which he cannot extricate himself. In a flowery style, entirely uncharacteristic of Devlin, he says that he is falling madly in love, that he has succumbed to uncontrollable passion.

> *Was that cannon fire? Or is it my heart pounding? Oh i guess it's my heart racing for you sweetheart. It started yesterday evening. You got my heart beating faster and slower at the same time which is a good thing. Trust me you are different from every other ladies I've come across with in my entire life, i can feel the flow of our love across which is really strange but i love the feelings.*

This email is so overwhelming that the doubt flips through my consciousness. I wonder if Devlin was really the author of this message at all. Then I brush aside my doubts. Perhaps he has been affected by his experience of me. It also occurs to me that a woman has written this email. This idea I quickly banish from my consciousness: This cannot be.

A day after the "falling into a canyon" message I receive a paragraph that is so somber, so censorious, and in so unique a style for Devlin that I turn numb in disbelief. It bears no resemblance to the "Dear Sunshine" or the "Sweetheart" emails. It does not invoke the canyon metaphor; it does not acknowledge any passion between us. It amounts to a stern admonition. It is as if I were being given my marching orders.

Keep secrets told to you. Never tell someone's story if i would not want it told. This is a betrayal of trust, and whatever we shared should be between us. I do not want a third party to get involve with our private life … because the tendency is to let things slip when you are under pressure, tired, or not thinking clearly, so we should always keep our relationship closed about what we talk about or do for each other.

"Why would I talk about you?" I wonder. I do not like any one giving me orders, telling me what I can and cannot say. Still, I acquiesce. "Of course I'll abide by your wishes," I promise. It is way too late in my life for me to worry about my identity, my independence of mind and spirit, to pause on the outlandish moment of a man giving me orders. Idly, I remember that he is a stranger, after all, with an identity of his own. I spot yet another red flag waving in the distant breeze. I lie to myself. I pretend that I do not see this red flag. But apparently his ploy has worked. While I lived and breathed under the hypnotic power of "Michael Devlin" I did not mention his specious name.

* * *

I am now waking up at three in the morning to reach for my iPhone to check if there are any new emails. Only two and a half weeks have passed, and I am firmly under the spell of self-hypnosis. A calm has settled over me. I pronounce myself "happy" if to only myself. I feel as if I know his voice, although I have never heard it.

I ask if his illness is completely gone. I admit that I have censored myself and so have not used the word "overdo." "Please take the long view," I say, "and protect yourself."

"I feel superb today. Sunshine," he answers. "Thanks for caring. I really appreciate it." This is followed by an emoji. I can't make out the expression on its face. Truth be told, they all look alike to me.

"I hope you have a wonderful night rest, can't wait to receive a text from you in the morning, Sunshine," is how he closes the day's communications, "Sweet dreams, kisses."

This is followed by another Emoji and a line of plump red lips.

June 22nd: "Although it was raining here this afternoon and it really affected us while working today," Devlin writes. "Really miss you so much today." His emails still close on "Michael Devlin – Chat @ Spike."

I am talking too much. "I couldn't sleep most of the night, tossing and turning," I write, "walking around. It's a good thing I don't have your telephone number, because the last thing you need is someone waking you up. I appreciate everything," I say, "and I am grateful. You are unique for me. Once in a while, it's overwhelming, which is not a bad thing. I hope the vestiges of your illness are all gone. You are in my heart." I ask him for a virtual hug. I have taken leave of my sanity.

Even to myself I sound sappy.

"Thanks for caring," Devlin says. "I really appreciate." He sounds like an NBA player in a post-game interview, bored but fulfilling his obligation. When he doesn't reply right away, still he apologizes. "I was so exhausted yesterday," he says, "next thing I knew I had drifted off to sleep."

It seems as if we are a couple chafing at being apart. At 7:49 the next morning he writes: "You have no idea how happy I am receiving a text from you. Life has never been better thanks to you, Sunshine. Well, I'm just relaxing here this morning and having my coffee. How was your night, Sunshine? I hope you slept good."

"You are so sweet, Sunshine," he writes the next day. Then he adds, "I'm feeling a lot better every day." This is followed by a profusion of red lips mixed with Emoji faces.

"I am collecting those kisses to cash them in for real kisses when the time comes," I dare say. In my deepest heart I doubt that the time will ever come. But I fortify myself with hope. *You never know.*

On this cloudy June morning, he refers to me as a writer for the first time. "Has anyone ever told you how great you write? I get goosebumps reading some of your mails." This gives me no pleasure, for reasons I cannot fathom. I had always fantasized that someone would fall for me for my writing. Martin F. Dardis told me he fell in love with my author photograph on the jacket of *Hellman and Hammett*. That turned out to be partly true, or temporarily true. I attributed it all to that great photographer of authors, Jerry Bauer.

"Any not anything stupid keyboard" Devlin suddenly writes apropos of I know not what. Meanwhile I have become obsessed with the absence of correct English grammar and punctuation in his messages.

* * *

It has been decades since I first confronted the rebellion against Standard English grammar among undergraduates and graduate students alike. It was as if ignoring my corrections was a political act. Firm in their ideology was the insistence on substituting "like" for "as." At first I held staunchly to the rules. After a few years I didn't care anymore. More recently they seem to have reverted to the old ways. Perhaps the renewal of correct English came with the shrinking of the publishing industry and how difficult it had become to be published. These students were nothing if not practical.

Structure was not even the worst problem. Year after year it became apparent that they had never mastered a political vocabulary. I was astonished when an undergraduate confessed that he had never heard of Dwight David Eisenhower. They had not developed critical thinking, and so were not prepared to assess Barack Obama's presidency.

* * *

None of Devlin's emails made any reference to any political or historical figures. It was as if he were one of my students. I was never to discover how old he was. The grey hair might have been misleading. Surely he could not have been a member of Generation Z?

For the slightest glitch, I had begun to blame myself. "Please wake up and send me a hug (virtual is ok)," I write. "If

I said anything offensive, please forgive me. I am sorry. You are in my heart." I cannot recall what inspired this mea culpa. I did not predict what was coming.

I never asked Devlin why he had chosen me. I remember a moment in one of Irving Howe's graduate seminars at the City University of New York. He was talking about the Holocaust, and his searing anecdote featured Dr. Primo Levi newly arrived at Auschwitz concentration camp. Levi could not comprehend the reason for this fiendish mass murder. A man of science, Levi required an explanation.

"Why are you doing this?" was, in effect, Levi's question. Surely there must be a rationale for such cruelty.

The young guard to whom Levi addressed his question was clear-eyed.

"Here there is no why," he said.

Sitting there in CUNY's Madison Avenue temporary housing around a shabby wooden table, a chill ran down my spine as Professor Howe related that story to his class on "The Idea of the Modern."

But Howe's anecdote turns out to be a mantra for millennial America. "The big question is why," says a catfish victim on MTV.

One catfish, confronted with his cruelty, says he feels no remorse, "because it wasn't real." A catfish based in Africa justifies his deception because catfishing, stealing money from victims, is his job supporting him and his girlfriend. Addressing only Americans, he makes between two and three hundred dollars a month. Should a victim balk and not turn over the money, "Frank" simply blocks her from communications and moves on to the next name on his list. "I am not financially stable," this catfish explains. That he was causing pain to others doesn't even occur to him.

"No, I'm not angry with you, Sunshine," Devlin says. "Why would I be? I didn't see your text till this morning. Trust me when I said my phone is really acting up lately. Just got up and I'm glad we're not working today. How was your night, Sunshine?

"You can do a background check on me if you want to,"
he adds, suddenly. "I don't mind." It occurs to me at once
that I don't have enough information to initiate such a check.
Then he adds, "I haven't been using social media for long.
It distracts me from so many things like my job, reading,
and some other tasks that I have to do on time. My days are
all planned out with work. I get up in the morning, take my
shower, have my coffee, and then start working, probably
will be done by 5:30 or 6, relax after dinner, then catch up
on some reading before I get on here."

He doesn't mention that he is in daily communication with
anyone else, not even his daughter. Her reality dims for me.
I don't know what social media has to do with background
checks, but perhaps I am simply behind the times.

He talks a lot about the weather these days. On June 23rd
he writes: "It's cloudy here this morning and pretty chill. The
weather forecast says it's gonna be raining here this afternoon and I really hate working in the rain."

His other favorite subject is technology. "About your last
text," he writes on June 23 at 4:52 am, "I could barely receive
notification until I enter my mail. Assuming it was google
chat, I could receive a text from you anytime, I know this way
of messaging you is kinda difficult, but it's just the mean-
time. I apologize for my late response, Sunshine. I will try to
get this notification issue fixed."

On June 23rd, at 7:54 pm, he writes, "For weeks now, when
it was time to sleep, I'd always think of you. It just seems that
I can't imagine a life without you anymore, Sunshine."

Could this be true? Has my life changed so dramatically
as now to include a person of such enthusiasm and apparent devotion?

* * *

There are now several generations that don't draw any
distinction between what is real and what is virtual. A local
lawyer out here introduced himself to new clients via Zoom.
It is much easier to cheat people when they have no opportunity to look you in the eye and ask, what do you plan to do

for us? A group of neighbors, attempting to thwart a project of building two McMansions on a small property in a pretty rural area, chipped in for a retainer to pay a lawyer who did nothing for our case. There was no law against his malfeasance. He did return about half the retainer, and we should consider ourselves fortunate.

Who would not then subscribe to Voltaire's suggestion that we cultivate our own gardens, literally and figuratively? We all have gardens, and we are all victims of a catfishing lawyer. Any one of the four of us might echo a line spoken frequently on *"Catfish"*: *"I SHOULD HAVE KNOWN BETTER."*

* * *

"I'm feeling a lot better today, Sunshine, and thanks to you for your encouraging text," he says, "tbh." I assume this means "to be honest," but I can't be sure. I would ask Audrey but she's not around. Her sweet dad has died suddenly of Parkinson's, which seems to have risen to epidemic proportions with no cure in sight.

"I really can't wait for five weeks anymore just to be with you," Devlin writes. This email is accompanied by one set of lips and one emoji face. I can't tell if the emoji is sad, with blue tears. Or smiling. His mention of a time limit renews my fear of whether he will like me, how I look, how he expects me to look. It does not occur to me that it is well-nigh impossible for us to meet, let alone that we will never meet at all. I wonder whether he might not have the money to come East. Was he homeless? Penniless? Was he able to support himself?

* * *

"I would like to hear your voice," I write at 10:22 on the evening of June 23. "Is that wrong?" I return to an earlier thought. I wonder whether my assumption that his being in Cuba restricts our communication was simply false. He had managed to convince me that he could not telephone me from Cuba without his having to lie.

"I would love to hear yours also," he replies. "Just bear with me. My network carrier is still not working. It's not supposed to take this long for a roaming network service, not sure why mine is taking forever. I will ask one of my crewmen for help because I'm not too savvy with this whole stuff."

I don't know what he is talking about. Then he adds: "For weeks now when it was time to sleep, I'd always think of you. It just seems that I can't imagine a life without you anymore, Sunshine."

There is now such a flurry of emails that it seems as if we are together day and night, bound by such strong feelings that they transcend practicalities.

I go to the doctor, and Devlin seems concerned. He wants to know what kind of doctor it was. I describe my scratchy eyelid; it is an eye doctor. "Did you have "Lasik" surgery?" Devlin asks. What is "Lasik surgery?" I wonder. The opthamologist tells me to come back in a year.

I feel a need to appear strong and without maladies, as if I were auditioning for a role in his life.

I tell him that I am watching the NBA draft, an event rarely missed by basketball aficionados. I note that this sport never elicits a response from him. Once more it occurs to me that he may not be an American at all. Yet NBA games are broadcast in many countries.

"I hope you have a wonderful night's rest," Devlin closes out this day.

"Really miss you so much today," he adds. "I can't wait to be with you this summer beneath the trees, learning from each other and growing in love." I am now certain we are looking at a real future. I am calm. It's just a matter of time, isn't it?

"My trees or yours?" I rejoin.

Time, that hidden indefatigable enemy of love, stretches before me unbroken. Or so I tell myself.

"Of course you do know I meant my trees where I live, LOL," he says. I have no idea of where he lives. There were no trees in any of the photographs he sent ostensibly picturing him at home in Arizona. Still, I believe that the day we will be together has been determined for history and is drawing ever closer. Nothing like this has ever happened to me before.

I tell him that I find him, "...most definitely lovable and a serious person too. I am impressed," I say.

It is June 24th. "I feel superb today, Sunshine," he says. He is now more fulsome. "For weeks now," he says, "when it was time to sleep, I'd always think of you. It just seems that I can't imagine a life without you anymore, Sunshine." I don't allow myself to notice that he is repeating himself, as if he were working from a preconceived, and limited, repertoire.

I tell him that I fear he will be disappointed if he meets me. "I'm not perfect," I say.

"Trust me, Sunshine," he replies. "I definitely know we are perfectly imperfect. I know this may all sound bizarre to you. But do you have any idea how much I like you?"

"There are a few things I need to tell you," I say. "I didn't think we were at that point. No, I'm not dying of AIDS or cancer or a heart ailment. But I thought you were a person to whom impediments didn't matter. Isn't it better if I just mention that I'm not perfect?"

I don't believe this at all.

At this point, I don't know what I believe.

"Thanks for caring," Devlin repeats. "I really appreciate."

It did not occur to me that he was not real. I sense that I must accept reality as he defines it. I realize that in Internet culture you are not entitled to know the people who turn up on your Facebook page. It is a less civilized world than the one in which I grew up. The old expectations will not be honored. In this newly evolved society, I felt unsettled and out of place. The new rules didn't rule Devlin out. They ruled ME out. I thought I was living in the world in which I was born. I wasn't. My awakening was rude and seemed to go on forever.

He sends me a photograph of himself on a motorcycle. He is not the dashing logger now. He looks like one of the many boyfriends of my childhood friend, beautiful blonde Audrey Bell, a full-blown woman at the age of thirteen with her tight fuchsia orlon sweater and massive breasts who hung out with boys in black leather jackets, cigarettes dangling from their lips. The lone girl, Audrey, stood fearless among them, commanding attention at the corner of 169th Street at the top of a bleak hill in the Bronx on a street where there were no trees.

* * *

It was Audrey Bell, an aficionado of the Roller Derby, who described for me the mechanics of sexual intercourse. We were in the fifth grade, out of school and home for lunch, as we were every day on Grant Avenue. We were older by a few years than kids today when they learn the facts of life. A parade of freckles marched across Audrey's small, flat nose.

I was horrified; surely this disgusting business couldn't be true. I wanted to ask my mother, but I didn't. I knew that what Audrey said had to be true. I can see us now, playfully calling each other "enemies." In our many encounters, Audrey expressed no malice. I studied harder; she was by far the better athlete, fearless and without errors. And how she could jump rope, a feat I could never accomplish!

I was intimidated by Audrey Bell. When she elected to take a commercial track rather than an academic one that would lead to college I was not surprised. I was, in fact, somewhat relieved and yet sorry at the same time. She was always smart, in the same "Special Progress" class that I was in, which meant that we both skipped the eighth grade. Junior high graduation day was the last day I would ever see her. She died young, I discovered, perhaps of the same cancer that claimed her mother, Clara Bell, who spent most of her days at the beauty parlor, nurturing her lacquered blond hair and long, blood-red fingernails. Once Clara gave me a permanent and left the mixture on too long so that my hair was a frizzy mess for months.

Audrey Bell died before I could learn to appreciate her.

* * *

Seeing the photograph of Devlin on a motorcycle, I tell him that he looks like a thug. I knew full well that not everyone was like those 50s juvenile delinquents who hung out with Audrey Bell smoking marijuana, but I say it anyway. Sitting on that bike with a mischievous grin on his face, he assumed another identity entirely, a person with whom I had no acquaintance.

"That was three years ago," he says, suggesting that he is a different person now. Along with Devlin on the bike are photographs of two tall beautiful blonde women standing with Devlin at a barbecue. I wonder who they are. Then I dismiss the thought.

Now he sends a picture of a bouquet of red roses. I believe this portends the arrival of a bunch of real roses, but I am wrong. It means nothing more than the photograph. It still does not occur to me that there will be no real roses, not now, not ever. I remind myself that Devlin does not know my address or telephone number. How was he to send anything even if he wanted to?

I, who abhor lying, lie to myself: I still believe that sooner or later I will meet Michael Devlin. Maybe even this coming summer. Then I will cash in on those emojis, which I have come to interpret as promised kisses.

In a romantic frame of mind, I write Devlin a long email about my favorite novel about love, the aforementioned *Love In The Time of Cholera* by Gabriel García Márquez. After fifty years of their being apart, an elderly man and a newly minted widow, whom he has loved all his life, are sailing down the Magdalena River, alone at last. She has overcome her shyness, her apprehension that her seventy-year-old body will surely not please him. It has been a long time since she has been the slender girl with whom he fell in love.

To facilitate their love, the Captain has hoisted the yellow flag denoting that there is cholera aboard. The law demands that all strangers be so warned lest they come aboard and be infected.

But there is no cholera stalking this boat, only the inevitabilities of life that can be softened (but not avoided) only by Florentino Ariza's lifelong undying love and Fermina Daza's growing affection. I compare our feelings for each other to the bond between Florentino Ariza and Fermina Daza. Devlin does not respond, is not touched by the analogy. He has never heard of García Márquez or of this masterpiece of eternal love. He evinces no further curiosity. Millions across continents have rejoiced in these novels, including *One Hundred Years of Solitude*, but the door to Devlin's heart is closed to great literature.

* * *

"You with your mind," an exasperated friend shouts over the phone, "how could you fall for this?"

Her words alienate me and turn me against her. I am completely smitten. I lie in my hot lonely bed, and he is lying there beside me. I feel his physical presence, I can feel his soft breaths. I touch my face and it is burning hot. Sexual desire washes over me, waves of longing that I have never in all my life experienced even in the company of very attractive men, men fair and sinewy who were in my style.

He is stretched out beside me. He is palpable, I could touch him if I wanted to. But I don't. I just want to lie here immobile. It is enough that he is here with me, that he exists. He is breathing steadily, quietly. There is no trace of a conflict between us. The only thing that matters is that we are both alive at this moment and that we have found each other. It is not conceivable that we should be lost to each other. My mind cannot penetrate a space empty of his existence.

I touch my face again and it is burning hot. Desire now roars through my body, originating from the top of my head. My body is now open as it has not been since the 1960's. One term I have rarely enlisted is "happiness." I feel as if I am experiencing what it means to be happy for the first time in memory. I offer no analysis. I just knew I was happy. If Devlin said I was beautiful, it must be true. His affection has transformed me into a lovable person. Anything is possible.

I am all aglow and it matters not a whit that I have never met this man, that I have never heard his voice. If this should have been a red flag, I didn't notice it. Devlin could not possibly be a person of deformed consciousness capable of senseless cruelty, like the roaming Catfish who torture their victims on the MTV series.

* * *

On June 24th I ask, "Did you ever take a peek at my website?" Then I add, again, "I am trying not to be a disappointment."

My final email of June 24th is a paean to him. "These emails are very strong and loving," I write. "Maybe that's all we need."

* * *

On Sunday, June 25th, I am invited to a baseball game at Citizens Bank Park in Philadelphia. I am with Audrey and her husband Alex. We are seated in the mezzanine looking down on a cracker box of a field, a far cry from the old Yankee Stadium where I spent many a Saturday afternoon of my childhood with my best friend Ronnie.

Saturday was Ladies Day, so we got in for fifty cents. The grandstands were shiny and green, everything pristine. After the game, like everyone else, we walked across the grass to the Monuments to Ruth, Gehrig, and DiMaggio, a quasi-religious pilgrimage, solemn and holding us to the highest standard of good behavior.

Today we seem to have landed in a mini-baseball park. Everything is shabby. The food is dry and tasteless. Certainly, there are none of the poké boxes with fresh tuna you can find at the Mets' Citi Field, only stale hot dogs wrapped in tin foil. Audrey and Alex are rooting for the Phillies. I am on the mezzanine among a few scattered Mets fans. Yet, I feel as if I am safely in a bubble and Devlin is inside with me. I am happy.

Before leaving for the game, I write to him. I tell him where I am headed. I will not wear my bright orange Jacob de Grom T-shirt, I say, because there is a very rough crowd here. I am thinking of a time Ralph went to a game in Philadelphia wearing a blue NY Mets T-shirt, and on his way out of the ballpark a fan slammed a punch into the side of his head. The world has been turned upside down. Today's crowd is docile, if not exactly knowledgeable about baseball. They cheer wildly for every high fly ball hit in the direction of the outfield as if it were a grand slam home run.

* * *

I tell Devlin that I once wrote a book about Bob Knight. "I don't care about what people think about what I do," I say. "Of course, I got hammered for that one."

I write that I like the ESPN sports analysis program "Pardon the Interruption" adding that one of the hosts lives in Arizona, and there are cactus in the background when he speaks.

"I hope you enjoy your sport game, honey," Devlin says. "Just leave a text when you get home. Love ya."

Sherlock interviewing the late Bob Knight, Indiana University, the basement of Assembly Hall, Bloomington, Indiana, 1987.

Who do you think I rooted for?" I ask Devlin playfully. But on this June 25th, what he wants to talk about is not baseball, but love.

"The best love," he writes, "is the kind that awakens the soul and makes us reach for more, that plants a fire in our hearts and brings peace to our minds. And that's what you've given me. That's what I'd hoped to give you forever." He closes with an emoji of one red heart.

"This is dazzlingly sweet," I answer. "What is bizarre is that we should both feel like this at the same time." Then I continue. "What added to my trust was when you told me that near the end of her life, your mother gave herself to Christ."

This touches his soul. "Aww sweet [heart emoji], I really can't wait to be with you anymore. I want all of you forever, Sunshine, you and me every day … I'll smile at you with joy."

When I repeat that I fear he will be disappointed, he has a ready reply. "Do you have any idea how much I like you? I had no intention of falling for you, but you made me love again. You've brought back those hopes and dreams to my life once again. A few months ago, I was thinking of how to start a new job after my retirement, but all I could think was looking forward to the future with you in it."

This was followed by a hopeful emoji. Does the person to whom I am writing feel more comfortable with little cartoon emojis than with language? Grey hair and goatee or not, is he in his thirties? Surely, he is not of my generation.

"I'm glad your team won," Devlin says, and I realize that he was not reading my messages, because on that day the Phillies demolished the Mets. He does not acknowledge the Mets, as if he has never heard of them. All I can think is that even if he had grown up in Lafayette, Louisiana, as he claimed, he would have heard of the Mets, if only to register his contempt.

This game turned out to be the season's turning point for the Mets. Having held their own for seven innings, for no rhyme or reason, suddenly and with determination they self-destructed, losing in a flurry of errors and bad base-running. For a Mets fan, this game was excruciatingly unwatchable. As the game ended, in a fit of disappointment, despair and disgust, the sky opened and thrust down thick sheets of cold, angry rain. We cannot reach our automobile without being soaked through.

It is only June 25, but the Mets are done for the season. In short order they will pack up and ship off their two-star pitchers, Max Scherzer and Justin Verlander, in so orchestrated a scenario that it seems like a conspiracy. At once the spirit of the team is broken. Their star position player, Pete Alonso, will bat .221 for the season.

* * *

At 5:42 AM on June 26th, Devlin writes, apologizing for not getting back to me "yesterday." He still believes that "my team" won the game. "Which is a double YAY! Am glad you had wonderful time yesterday." To demonstrate that he did read my email, he writes: "I'm sorry you got wet yesterday. Hope you didn't get cold?"

"Thinking about you," he writes, adding an emoji of a heart. "Hurry up and wake up, honey, coz miss you so much."

63

This is followed by an emoji of a perplexed face, its eyebrows twisted in opposite directions.

At 12:13, I write back the saccharine "Good morning, dear one." Then, for no reason available to me, I launch into a riff on hard work. "Either you work very hard or nothing valuable gets done," I begin, boring even myself. "Try telling most students that." Devlin has never made a reference to my having spent my life as a teacher, yet I keep dragging in this subject. This must be who I am. It does seem odd that he does not respond to the moments when I share with him impressions gleaned from a lifetime of teaching.

* * *

During my fifty years in university classrooms, I sometimes asked students why they wanted to be writers. The question was unwelcome and closed rather than welcomed further discussion. Almost no one voiced an ambition. What I concluded was that calling yourself a writer conferred an identity, an overrated concept in my view, although I never said that.

Over the years, I found that teachers attached to creative writing programs, including our own, had become silent enforcers of the political status quo. As a student, so long as your stories did not challenge the social structure, so long as your characters fixated on their personal lives, and you as the author kept them rooted in their individuality, you were safe. You would excel in the program, and you would be awarded fellowships, or, at the very least continuing financial aid. In the case of one fellowship, the program director had to co-sign a student's application. He refused, only for me to call him out. He backed away, and the student received the award. She saw nothing unusual in this, but I did. Surely independence of mind has become an underrated virtue.

It took me some years to figure out that confirming the status quo had been infused into creative writing programs from the early days of the Cold War. Radical change was inconceivable. Only after decades did I learn that this political blanket had been smothering the programs since the last days of World War Two, first at Iowa, the premier program in the country, and then at Stanford. Hiring was influenced – enabled – by CIA-inflected institutions like the Rockefeller Foundation that dispensed munificent grants to anti-communist journals, and international conferences, although surely not the one attended by Pat Moriarity and me at Long Island University.

A more likely CIA target was Princeton University, which garnered a multi-year grant of $100,000 to fund its Gauss seminars in literary criticism, some of which I attended as a local resident. One was given by a writer named Julia Kristeva, known as a Marxist, but not resembling any leftist I had ever heard of.

Writers in the creative writing programs were expected to write fiction, and rarely did Temple allow me to offer a course in non-fiction writing. The students knew they were not supposed to be writing non-fiction. The Gauss Seminars made me uncomfortable, a feeling I attributed to a sense of class inferiority in the Princeton landscape. I was to blame. I was not good enough.

Sherlock at Princeton Library, Princeton, New Jersey, 2006.

"If your central motive is to put across ideas," Steve Almond, who frequented the creative writing circuit, pontificated, "write an essay." Paul Engle at Iowa had framed the fiction workshop "as a whole as a quiescent entity crucial to a liberal democratic capitalistic America." So, these CIA assets outlined their cold war agenda for both creative writing students and their fictional characters. Lurking behind this enterprise was the containment of Communism and the repudiation of American radicalism in any form.

My students – we began the creative writing program in the mid-1980s – didn't have to be told the parameters. They knew before I did. After a while I noticed that they almost never set their stories in foreign countries. Topical political issues were unthinkable and were not considered as a source of characterization.

I organized a seminar on "Setting" to encourage the class to focus on this least developed aspect of fiction writing. There were exceptions. Eduardo Bechara, a Colombian lawyer and now a poet and related to the tennis star Martina Navratilova, set a novel in post-World War Two Czechoslovakia. Rachel Howe set her novella in Israel as she chronicled a love story between an American woman on a kibbutz and a Palestinian man, and for the Setting course that was it as far as their setting their novellas in the wider world was concerned.

None of the faculty referred to any constrictions placed upon the students. No one told them what to write about, did they? At around this time, Donald Trump was elected to the presidency. That night some of my students marched down Broad Street in protest. What they didn't like about Trump was what they perceived as his racism. But their effort dissipated. They seemed to lack the moral stamina to build a movement. By the time I had retired in July 2019, the leadership of the program had regressed so much that its culture seemed not like political censorship, but mere mediocrity.

I was struggling on other fronts. At an NYU conference about terrorism, I ran into the *New York Times* columnist Anthony Lewis, whose subject was the first amendment. By way of introducing myself, I mentioned that I was writing a biography of Jim Garrison. A small, slim figure all in black, Lewis turned visibly pale. Then he slipped out the nearest door. I knew that the *New York Times* had published the Warren Report with an introduction by Lewis, but it hadn't occurred to me that they would not review a book about Garrison, the leading critic of the Warren Report at the time, because of a position they had taken two decades in the past.

Not that the *Times* was the only institution to look askance at a book about Garrison. CIA released a document in April

1967 instructing reviewers to write that those who criticized the Warren report were in fact agents of the Soviet KGB. This document does not mention Garrison by name. Nor does it acknowledge Lee Harvey Oswald's movements around the state of Louisiana during the summer of 1963. Garrison remarked more than once that everyone observed in Oswald's company was in some way connected with CIA. Garrison's primary suspect, a CIA contract pilot, had recruited Oswald into the Civil Air Patrol when Oswald was a teenager. It was all connected, as Don DeLillo noticed in his brillant novel, *Libra*.

* * *

It is all mundane now as I must correct Devlin that "my" team did not win that game yesterday. "After sitting there for nearly five hours, I watched as the Mets threw the game away." I move then into our familiar territory. I tell him how I love waking up and finding a message from him. "It changes my day," I confide. "Have you noticed that I am a shade spoiled?" I don't really believe this is true, but I can no longer distinguish between true and false.

On the day after the game, June 26, I still believe that we are together, that we had found each other, and that the world stretches before us as a couple. I call him "dear one" and report that I haven't caught a cold despite my having been thrust into the core of a raging storm. I tell him that I long for some warm cuddles.

He has been writing to me every day for more than three weeks and I am content with that. I have grown to expect to hear from him daily. His presence has become "normal," a term that by the middle of the 21st century has lost all meaning anyway. I have long since ignored his fraught acquaintance with the English language. I am well aware that he doesn't connect with references that any American would recognize. Among the references he doesn't "get" are: the New York Mets; my friend the late Bob Knight; the Kennedy assassination. He never asked me what my book about Cuba was about, casting doubt upon his claim to actually be in Cuba.

Now a day arrives when there is no message from him at all. I am alarmed. I panic. I expected the worst, and here it is. I fear that he has tired of me. I am too old, too boring. The seventies with its promises to women has been erased from history. I have disappointed a man, and that is all that matters.

This morning in the dead heat of the hottest of summers the air feels like ice on my skin. No word from Devlin after dinner either. The silence feels abnormal. Did I say something disappointing? When I have heard nothing by 6:00 PM, I am in despair. So it is over, I think. So this is the end, a line from Ozu's film *Tokyo Story* spoken by the recently dead old lady's husband. I still have never heard Devlin's voice.

The next morning, with nothing left to lose, I decide to write him one more email.

"Are you alright?" I say. I sense my weakness, that I am conscious that I am speaking through my hypnosis. Later in the evening three photographs arrive. They are panoramic views of a logging accident. One is filled with smoke. Firefighters crawl across the lndscape. In another sits an abandoned broken-down harvester. In the third you can glimpse a slender man with blond  hair; he wears tight blue jeans as he surveys the scene. He is too far from the camera to be recognizable. It may or may not be Devlin. In the third picture, two men are pulling a third from some wreckage.

One of his crew has been taken to the hospital, Devlin writes. I remark inanely on the excellence of the Cuban health care system.

"What can I do to help?" I write.

Devlin reappears the next day, confiding that he is "in trouble." He cannot afford to rent or to buy a replacement harvester. He says that he brought $200,000 with him. But it isn't enough. He is in danger of losing his contract with the Cubans. This will thwart his coming retirement. His entire future is at stake. A 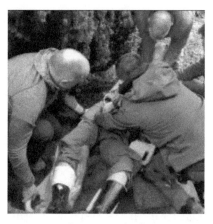 friend has given him $35,000. From me, he *needs* $15,000.

All I can see on the page is a parade of zeros. I feel as if I've been tossed into a bathtub of ice cubes, paralyzing, sobering, deadening. Later, I recall Nev, I recall Max, asking female "catfish" victims, "Have you ever sent him money?" "Has he ever asked you for money?" On one episode a victim tells Kamie, Max's replacement, that she sent the man catfishing her "a grand."

"That's a lot of money," Kamie says.

On the *Catfish* show, where victims are scarcely out of their adolescence, they have lost only hundreds of dollars. One sends forty dollars to be used for gas money. $300 is sent to replace a broken cell phone. Excuses from the exposed catfish are banal. Most are of the variety of "no one ever cared about me," as if this were a justification for perfidy.

Devlin refers to having telephoned Havana. It doesn't occur to me even now to request that he phone me. "Not having a phone conversation is always bad," Nev once remarked. I can hear Max adding, "This is how most people meet these days."

Devlin now reveals a level of self-pity of which I didn't expect any man was capable.

"You are the only person I can turn to," he writes. "My life will be miserable." He is sounding suicidal, something I have never heard from him.

It occurs to me to send him the $15,000, if only to demonstrate that I don't deserve any better. Yes, in a paroxysm of self-hatred, as punishment for believing that I could have a life with this man, I decided to send him the $15,000. If it had all been about money, then let it be about money. I had never heard this man's voice; I had never so much touched his hand or looked into his eyes. I had no idea of how many women he was subjecting to this scam. But, truth be told, I could access this cash easily. I believed that only if I punished myself for this folly, this delusion, the fantasy that I could ever be happy, would I be at peace.

It came back to me that the Devlin emails had come in a variety of styles. Some were spare and to the point. Others were flowery to the point of nausea, almost as if the writer were enjoying the ugly scam.

I wrote, "How do I get this money to you?" He knew I had no contact information for him, no address, no phone number. Was he surprised that I was moving ahead so quickly? Then I can't help myself, I say, "Both of us probably know that if you and I had ever met, you would not like me much. Still, I'm going to say yes, the price to me of your kind words and emails. Nothing comes for free. I believe I deserve the same honesty I gave you." *That was not to be.*

As any accomplished catfish would know, time was now of the essence. In seconds, I have a well-organized, formal, business-like reply, the culmination of my sorry romantic adventure. Here are the instructions on how I was to get the money to Michael Devlin. Note that this message offers no information as to where he is geographically. It is June 29th at 5:15 pm when I receive this set of instructions to present to my bank in order that they may wire the $15,000.

* * *

"Patelco Credit Union
3 Park Place
Dublin, California 94568
Account name: Tajay Edgerson
Address: 2620 Wyandotte Street, Apt. 9

Las Vegas, Nevada 89102
#74600506462110
Routing # 321076470"

• • •

"Thank you so much honey, you are such a sweetheart," Devlin replies immediately, with an emoji heart followed by three emoji faces. "You have no idea how you have brought smile [incoherence in the original] to my face for helping me through this difficult time. I love you so much." This is followed by two more hearts and three emoji faces.

But my heart has turned to ice. "Who is Tajay Edgerson?" I ask. Devlin has never mentioned such a person.

"A collegue," he writes, indifferent to correct English spelling as he has always been. But Tajay can be found on LinkedIn, working at Caesar's Entertainment in Las Vegas, her duties to "maintain a working knowledge of availability, qualifying criteria, room rates, types, locations, package plans, special features, information on all outlets, hours of operation, respond to guest request for reservations." Previously she did similar work for a place called The Dragons Emporium. In her photograph she looks to be between 25 and 35. There had to be a real-life Tajay for the bank to extract the money.

* * *

As Nev notes on *Catfish*, there is always a "friend" waiting to receive the money. Requesting that money be sent through a friend is shady, Nev notes.

> Never send money to anyone you have only communicated with online or by phone," the FBI warns. On the

FBI website you will find the story of a woman who lost two million dollars to an online suitor she had never met. The FBI points out that scam artists often say they are in the building and construction industry and are engaged in projects outside the US. That makes it easier to avoid meeting in person – and more plausible when they ask for money for a medical emergency or unexpected legal fee.

The scammer's intention is to establish a relationship as quickly as possible, endear himself to the victim, and gain trust. Scammers may propose marriage and make plans to meet in person, but that will never happen. Eventually they will ask for money.

The FBI takes no prisoners. "Romance scams occur when a criminal adopts a fake online identity to gain a victim's affection and trust. The scammer then uses the illusion of a romantic or close relationship to manipulate and/or steal from the victim."

Homeland Security reports the story of a woman named Deborah who "fell hard when she met her Spanish lumberjack on a dating site in the middle of the COVID-19 pandemic." So lumberjack turns out to be a popular job for romance scammers. Homeland Security has statistics too: in 2020, older adults reportedly lost nearly $139 million dollars. In 2020 people in general lost $304 million to romance scams. Much was lost via the then popular cryptocurrencies.

"Be suspicious if you haven't met in person," Homeland Security and the FBI both warn repeatedly. As Devlin wanted me to transfer to Google Chat and made a considerable effort to get me to do it, Homeland Security warns, "Don't let the individual rush you to leave a dating service or social media site to communicate directly."

* * *

How is Tajay connected to Devlin's logging contract? Disrespectfully, he provides no details, he who accused a former lover of "disrespect." But in the penultimate hour, the scam is unraveling.

It is already June 29. Their deadline with me must be June 30. Who was masterminding this scam I have no idea, as I could never verify whether Devlin was ever in Cuba. I doubted whether individual Americans contracted with the Cuban government, but I did not know for sure.

I am shaken by his asking me for money, I feel like such a fool that I conclude not only that he does not care for me, but that he hates me. Surely had he cared for me at all, he would have protected me from being stripped of thousands of dollars, my hard-earned money. I think of the hundreds of hours (or is it thousands?) that I have devoted over many years to student stories and essays. Where does Devlin think the money came from? Vaguely, I wonder where my property tax money will come from in the coming quarter.

June 29 at 1:42 PM I write the first of several farewell messages to "Michael Devlin": "I believe that you hate me, and are laughing at me, how easily I was fooled. As I wrote in my last email, if you ever had the chance to meet me, you would not be impressed. I am not pretty like the women in the photographs in the group with the motorcycle. I am ordinary. My father's last words to me were, "You were never pretty." *That's neither here nor there.*

"I am not rich. What little money I have is some savings which I am sending to you because I hate myself for caring for you, and I did care. Now I doubt everything. IF you were raised in Louisiana, how come (emoji of a crawfish) etouffee didn't make your list? A bad joke, but the last. I'll call the bank now," I promise. I do wonder, why me? (Many of the victims on the *Catfish* program ask this question at the moment of their deepest distress).

I do call the bank. They resist. They do not want to send this money. They tell me that this transaction cannot be completed over the telephone. I must appear in person.

I explain all this to Devlin. Then I add, I cannot stop myself, "I must admit that I really fell for you. What a pity that it was not real. I will miss you. I wish you well. I know there are telephones in Cuba. My book was called *The Great Game in Cuba*. Ironic, isn't it?"

I was playing for time. I decided that were he to telephone me – it would be the first time – I would send him the money.

At 8:01 AM on June 30th, he replies in the normal way as if nothing were amiss, as for him it isn't, of course. "Seriously I just woke up to all this message," he writes. "I didn't get any notification. I really don't know what you are talking about. I really have no strength about all this honestly. Why are you saying all this, honey? Never in my life would I hate you. I'm in the middle of big mess yesterday and feel relieved when you said you're gonna help me out. This morning I just got the notification and my heart felt really down. Trust me, sweetheart," he says. "I'm not trying to fool you. Heavens no! Honey, please don't take this the wrong way." He feels close to getting many thousands of my dollars into his hands.

But by now I am enlisting my own intuition. At the same time, I am hopelessly unable to distinguish what is real from what is fake. He reveals that he is not one to panic unnecessarily. He is still soft with me. "Honey," he writes, "It's your money. You have the right to do whatever you wanna do with it. Why don't you go to the bank today and do it yourself, Sweetie. I already told the investors I'm getting this done today. These people are very straightforward. What am I supposed to tell them if I can't meet up?

"Trust me, Babe, I'll never leave you," he promises. "I'm really so scared of everything right now. I'm scared of forfeiting this contract. I'm scared of losing you." Three emoji faces follow, a sad emoji followed by two even more sorrowful emojis.

"Honey, please, I'm begging you," Devlin writes. "Just find a way and get me out of this whole mess, my love." It appears that I am responsible for whatever happens to him. I feel ice slowly inching up over my heart, even as I cling to the fantasy.

At 11:12 AM he (or she, if it is a she) makes a final appeal for me to send cash money by wire.

The worst part of it, sweetheart, is the company I am working with are threatening to bridge my contract and file a lawsuit. I might end up getting nothing and also be sued by the company and ruin the reputation of my company. I've worked so much and I've invested a lot of money just to get this contract! Am gonna see it slip my finger. And all I have with me is $200,000 so I asked a colleague here to help me and he was only able to help me with $35,000 because he recently bought a house in California. That's why he was able to help me with that amount.

None of this makes any sense to me. It does occur to me that such an operation should have been supported by insurance. Cuba, after all, if he was in Cuba, was not situated on the planet Tralfamadore.

Devlin now sums up his situation, lest it not be clear.

Right now, I need $15,000 to add to the $235,000 to enable me to get the harvester. I have tried all I can to get the $15,000 but to no avail. Now I have no choice but to ask you for this help. I am ashamed to be asking you for this. I feel very ashamed but I have come to the end of the road and you are the only one I can ask for this help. Please, Sweetie, you have to help me even if you are going to give it to me with interest. I will pay you as soon as I get my paycheck.

Please help me because I have already signed the contract.

At 1:17 in the afternoon comes some no-nonsense Devlin. "And also, Sweetie," he writes, "send slip after sending it." This email is signed Michael Devlin. Still, I can't just walk away. And I had promised him this money. Surely I must keep my promise and send him the $15,000 that he claims will save his life, clear up his contract with the Cubans and provide him with the bona fides for his retirement in the coming year. Aren't I the only person who can help him?

Surely my integrity or what's left of it demands that I send him the money. My intellect gives way before need, his and mine both. It does occur to me that a man at retirement age should have closer friends, relatives, and contacts than a woman he has known for less than a month and whom he has never met in person. I brush these reservations aside. *I will send him this money.*

No, I don't admit to myself that the money is all that connects us now. The computer and the Internet are assuredly Devlin's friends.

My bank is a very small local branch of a much larger institution. I make an appointment to come in person the next morning. The manager himself comes on the line to respond to my second request that they wire $15,000 to a woman in Las Vegas. "How well do you know these people?" he asks me in banker style. By now, in the summer of 2023, Homeland Security and the FBI, working together, have alerted the banks to tell their customers that no matter how lovesick they may seem, under no circumstances must they comply with these requests for money.

"I have never met them," I admit.

When I wake up the next morning, I am enrobed by a cold burst of reality, and I cancel the appointment with the bank.

So there I am, exposed to myself, a self-hypnotized woman willing to send thousands of dollars to a seemingly kind man and one, oddly sane.

In the light of this day, I write to Devlin and tell him "There can be no financial component between us." Then I anticipate: "So if you plan to ask for less money, or ask for money again, please give up on that. If that means giving up on me, that's all right too."

My tone reminded me of how I addressed an errant student attempting to talk his way out of the transgression of handing in a plagiarized story based on *Fight Club*. My job was made easier that time because several of his classmates recognized the similarity to *Fight Club*. Some transgressions are unforgivable, and so as per university regulations, I flunked him for that course.

Women are constantly underestimated, and time does not soften that blow. This applies to Devlin apparently. "Obviously I could not abide by your demand that I not speak to anyone about you and me," I say. "One of my team works for the intelligence services, it's a diverse group of men and women, older and younger, *as if there were such an entity looking after me*. If you are on the up and up, I hope you will demonstrate that."

This of course was spoken out of fear. Some side of me now knew that I was dealing with people who operated outside the law. Of what they were capable I did not know then, and I don't know now. We were neither friends nor lovers, only Internet strangers, a rather ugly category of human interaction. It occurred to me later that if I had been younger, I might have been more forgiving.

In our final exchange, on the same day. Devlin begged me again to go to the bank and wire the money. I sign off, even now, begging that he come to his senses, forget about this unreasonable request and renew his hope to meet me if he is serious.

I turn out to be the only person in my world bedeviled by this scam. The tree surgeon who works occasionally on my property was sardonic. "With $15,000," he remarks, "we could fix up this place." Mark stands for the honest man saving trees and my home environment, unlike a logger who rapes forests and cuts trees. They are diametrical opposites even as both are in the business of trees.

Emails move gingerly. By the end of the day, Devlin seems not to have received the message that I would not be sending him the thousands of dollars. In his final email he pours forth all the epithets he knows. "Sunshine," "Sweetie," "Babe," "Honey" "Sweetheart" and a new one, "Queen," are all on display. I still love him, and I am still affected by these terms of endearment. Or perhaps he read my email and found the only recourse he had was to appeal to my love for him - which persisted.

If you had asked me on June 30th, I would have told you with certainty, *I love him still*.

CODA

I was not quite done. New Orleans police officer Robert Buras had not bestowed on me the nickname "Sherlock," for nothing, although I confess to a vain pleasure in receiving his Dear Sherlock emails. I want to find out from whom I received all those emails. It was proving too hairy, far too devastating to give up the fact that there was a real Michael Devlin writing to me with so much affection.

I tried to Google him, but there was no Michael Devlin in Thatcher, Arizona, a town of some 4,000 inhabitants. Searching further afield, I did find a soccer player, but in Europe. I was soon to locate a host of Michael Devlin's using Facebook. Many were athletes, but I had not heard of any of them. My acquaintance with professional sports was limited to baseball, basketball, and American football. The Michael Devlin who had written to me was not an athlete.

Using Google Maps and the address from the wiring instructions, a friend zeroes in on Tajay's apartment in Las Vegas. It turns out to be a shabby five story tenement with a canvas canopy over the entrance in a run-down part of town, post-World War Two era. I recognize it because I grew up in a similar environment. This was not the slick Las Vegas built by mobsters and their opportunistic cohort who had reached the end of their rope. It looked more like the Bronx at the moment when it was passing its prime.

How could Tajay be the "colleague" of a hard-working logger, she rising out of the lies and stink and corruption of Vegas? Could this be where Devlin actually lives and has been the whole time? Here, together, they trapped me in their ugly romantic game, whose purpose was to line their pockets with some ready cash? $15,000 was not much, but it was a start. Maybe he told her that I "would get over it," just as he dismissed that old girlfriend with the words, "she'll get over it."

The day, and then days, passed with no word from Devlin. He had vanished into the ether. He had failed every test I could devise, even tests I created unconsciously, tests created by the side of me under self-hypnosis. He had no interest in the Kennedy assassination. He never inquired what my book about Cuba was about. He had never demonstrated that he was in fact in Cuba. He said the team I rooted for must be the "Jackals," and I exposed him by mentioning the Mets, but that did not faze him in the least. He knew something I did not, that I would never hear from him again.

I could not reconcile the sweet guy with the dog named "Reagan" with the half-hysterical man demanding $15,000 to be wired to an exotic recipient in Las Vegas.

I tried to shut my heart tight although my purse was closed. This was easy because money had never meant anything to me and didn't now.

Neither Devlin nor Tajay ever extracted a cent from me.

* * *

The documentary filmmakers arrived. After we were done with talking about Duvalier and Haiti we turned to the matter of Devlin, real and false. They are millennials with perceptions light years from mine. They zero in on the photograph of Devlin sitting there in his rainbow socks behind the wheel of the logging machine. The producer does a reverse image search of the photograph of Devlin in the logging machine, but the search produces zero results. We do learn that the logging machine itself was manufactured in Romania, a place likely to do business with Cuba, FWIW, "for what it's worth."

Audrey did a reverse image search for all the photos we had of Devlin. She searched for Michael Devlin on Facebook, LinkedIn, Twitter (X), Instagram, and more. Once he figured out that you were on to him," she said, "he deleted his Facebook account."

"The man in the photos may be dead," she added.

The Haiti film's director notices pine trees. Is this really Cuba? The filmmakers are skeptical, raising eyebrows at Devlin's socks. I contact two Cuban friends. One is Eduardo Sánchez Rionda. From a prominent Cuban family, he is now a real estate executive in Key Biscayne, Florida. The other is the brilliant novelist Cristina Garcia, who is married to my friend Dr. Gary Aguilar. Both Cristina and Eduardo acknowledge that, yes, there are forests of pine trees in Cuba.

I have been thoroughly catfished, stuck in the mud, a lowly place from which there is no exit, although of course I did exit. I exited victorious too. Hurt but not mortally wounded.

"Chat @ Spike?" I was never to discover what this meant. It might have been a warning, reminiscent of Dante's over the portal to hell. "Abandon hope" should you be such a fool as to have found yourself here.

Even now I cannot believe it is over, that I will never talk to him, never hear his voice. I write several more emails, imploring him to get in touch with me. Surely this cannot be the end; surely we will talk and climb onto more sure footing away from Tajay and whomever else is hovering near. There is no reply.

I search for more clues. I examine my own Facebook profile and so discover a blown-up photograph of the cover of my book, *Blood in the Water*. That was the reason behind Devlin's choice of this book as the one in which he was most interested. As I discovered, he never intended to read any of my books or to consult my website or to meet me.

After that first day the name Reagan, dog or man, never surfaced in any of his emails. He never telephoned me, even in the darkest times when the $15,000 was supposedly a matter of life and death to him. They will tell you on *Catfish TV* that if the person will not telephone you, it is a good indication that the gender of the person is not what you expect. The person calling me "Sunshine" must have been a woman! It is the lowest of moments on *Catfish* when the victim discovers that the gender of the object of her affection is other than what she expected.

In my search to find Devlin I attempted to retrieve his cache of emails to me. Doesn't AOL stash your emails for at least five years? I have come upon such records. I could not get rid of them. Yet three months after Devlin disappeared, it seems his name had been banished from my computer. I could find no trace of him, except what I had already printed out. A guru on *Catfish* put it this way: "What you should expect from a catfish is a blank profile."

* * *

Dr. Phil has done programming about catfishing, which has become an epidemic among his audience members. He unearthed, originating in Nigeria, a forty-page handbook entitled "How to Make a White Woman Fall in Love With You." It is addressed to those who plan to practice catfishing, a manual of do's and don'ts.

"Go to those over 40," the anonymous author begins on the first page. "They are working; hence they have the money you need." In the first week, tell the woman she is beautiful. That is very important. Then go on from there."

The next step is research. The catfisher should check his victim's social media for information. Then the catfisher is advised: "You want to send something that will make her like you from the very first text, something that will make her open your message and her heart for you." Enter Reagan the dog!

Among the safe and useful subjects, as Devlin knew, was travel. "Where's the next place you want to visit??" the manual suggests that you ask, just as Devlin did.

There is also a list of scripted sentences. One is, "You've been running through my mind all day." Another is, "I smile thinking about you when I'm alone." The Nigerian urges you to sprinkle heart emojis through your text.

"Ask her about herself," the author advises under the category of Conversation. Another question is straight out of the Devlin playbook. "So, what do you like to do for fun these days?"

Should the catfish offer information about himself? "Keep it short," the author advises, "interesting things but don't talk about yourself too much." The reason is not spelled out, but it is obvious. The catfish might well blow his cover with too much detail. And there is even a list of compliments to offer. "The more I learn about you," Devlin said, "the more I fall."

There are many generics from which to choose. "You complete everything I've ever wanted in a woman," is another good compliment. "I have fun just being beside you doing nothing," which sounds a lot like Devlin when he addressed my depiction of the two of us, "in five years' time" in a cottage by the sea.

Two separate sections in the manual are devoted to how to ask for money. The headings are "How to Ask" and "Take your Time." The first piece of advice is, "Don't ask directly." The author specifies: "Ask without looking like you're asking." You must also, after a week of chatting, admit that you "have exhausted every means to get money." This is exactly the approach Devlin took. He had contributed $200,000 of his own money; he had that friend who had just bought a house in California. He claimed he had tried everyone before coming to me.

There are other small suggestions. "Keep the chat going for long before you ask for anything," is obvious but important. "It may be time consuming," the pseudonymous author allows, "but its [sic] totally worth it."

Among the "bonus tips" in the catfish manual are some scripted sentences such as, "Hope you had a great day today," a Devlin favorite. "What are you doing this weekend?" was adopted by Devlin verbatim. So was this one: "I always fall asleep with a smile on my face when I'm thinking about you." The most frequent epithets are "sweet" and "sunshine." "You're the sunshine that wipes away my frown" was too corny even for Devlin.

"We will never get apart," the manual suggests. "I miss you" is a standard. "You are my sunshine" evokes the song by Louisiana governor Jimmy Walker, famous for having built a "bridge to nowhere," but who also wrote that unforgettable song. This was pointed out to me by an important source for

A Farewell to Justice, Dr. Frank Silva, the leading psychiatrist in Baton Rouge. Frank Silva's country of birth was Cuba – all things are connected.

One piece of advice Devlin did not bother to take. The manual urges that all messages should be in perfect English grammar. The would-be catfisher should use an app called "Grammarly," which can be installed on your phone. Devlin's grammar was a mess, not least his errant spelling and punctuation.

Ah, the glories of the Internet. I wonder if Tajay wrote any of the Devlin emails for him, or did she steal Devlin's entire identity, so that "Devlin" never even knew of this scam. Or were they co-conspirators, with some emails being written by the hysterical Tajay, illiterate and excessive, like the one where Devlin describes himself as having slipped and fallen into a canyon of love.

Others were the handiwork of the sweet Devlin, who had a daughter and a dog named Reagan, a kind and good human being, who would never extort money from a woman he never met or even spoke to, and who, finally, never summoned the courage or the desire to telephone.

I love him still. My energy remains positive, alive, and powerful – and real even if I am in love with an imaginary man. My heart is full even if he does not and never did feel anything. Does it matter if he loves me? Does it even matter that he doesn't exist, although I saw photographs of a kindly man – photos stolen and used in this deception? Does it matter that there may exist a logger named Devlin, but that he never heard of me? This hurts the most.

Doesn't it count that I see his impish smiling face before me, that I remember him still, no matter that he is up and gone? That he never knew me or even liked me?

I am in love with the imaginary Devlin. He loves the ocean, he told me with genuine enthusiasm. He looks forward to life. I am not far behind, as he waits for me at the edge of the sea. The air between us sparkles with light and joy.

"Michael Devlin," whether you are really one of ninety-five profiles that turn up on Facebook under the name Devlin, whether you are actually a woman who blocked me when I tried to contact you again, or whether you are a mere con man following a script that was designed to extort thousands of dollars from me under the preposterous scheme of replacing a harvester that caught on fire in Cuba – *my heart goes out to you still*. I think of the familiar Irish prayer, even as Devlin had never admitted that he was Irish, despite the name. "May the road rise up to meet you. May the wind be always at your back. May the sun shine warm upon your face. May God hold you in the palm of His Hand."

* * *

Is there a Michael Devlin who walks in the boots of a gentle woodcutter?

It felt natural and it felt real, and yet, everyone agrees, had I given him the money, only then would he have stayed – if only to extract more money. It had indeed been too good to be true. He seemed to care about everything about me, and what wife, what woman summons such attention? He had been concerned with why I was visiting an eye doctor, and whether I had slept well. He said he didn't mind if I did a background check on him. He was always calm and appropriate, a grown-up.

I wanted to believe, and would have gone on believing, in his existence, forever. Then one day I Googled "logger." Up came an article from the *Atlantic Monthly*, an interview with a real logger named Chuck Carlson out of South Dakota. This was a place Devlin had never mentioned, yet there in the Black Hills, in the late 19th century, was the place where logging in the United States had been born. It was Devlin's story, without his acknowledgement, an American story, a story of the settling of the west.

By the year 1900, especially after gold was discovered in Deadwood Gulch, Custer became the center of the lumber industry. The lumber itself, yellow Ponderosa pine, was building-ready. And so, the West grew and prospered. Trees, of course, were one thing. The objective of most of these first settlers was to discover gold. The story is conveyed in photographs of the period displayed at the 1881 Courthouse Museum in Custer.

Once the settlers arrived in numbers, they needed homes, services, and jobs. By 1900, Custer was the center for the timber industry. The settlers first built log houses. Where Devlin's father fit into this scenario I was never to discover.

What astonished me was that in an article in the *Atlantic Monthly* magazine I discovered an expert example of plagiarism by the "Michael Devlin" with whom I had been corresponding. He had assumed the persona of Chuck Carlson and had spoken in his voice, word for word!

"I was working with my dad at a very young age" Carlson tells his interviewer, "cutting trees for Custer Sawmill, and I fell in love with logging." So, from this interview, Devlin fashioned his identity as a logger. Carlson describes logging as "the most dangerous job in America." So Devlin evolved the scam of the accident in Cuba and its aftermath. He also concocted a romance of the perils of logging that might appeal to a lonely, aging, urban woman to whom physical danger was exotic.

"You have to respect the job," Carlson says. "If you get careless, you can get hurt or get somebody else hurt. It's just something you have to stay on top of at all times … you have trees falling and equipment can roll over down the hill. I've had friends get hurt pretty bad doing this, and killed."

So Devlin the imaginary logger concocted the plot of his scam. What better than a logging accident putting one of his "crew" in a Cuban hospital to touch the heart of a politically left-wing woman? Not that Devlin appropriated Carlson's entire biography. Carlson had been married to the same woman for twenty-seven years and was devoted to his three daughters, two of whom were in college, the youngest of whom was already skilled at operating a "skidder."

"I feel really good about myself after working a hard day," Carlson confides to his interviewer. This was a line that might have been spoken by Devlin. Someone had constructed this fake logger and set him down in Cuba, a place his Internet conquests were unlikely to penetrate.

This example of male fortitude and stoicism fulfills a post-World War Two male ideal. It flourished in the Westerns of John Wayne and is with us still. "It's very, very hard work," Carlson concludes. "It's made for some people, and it's very demanding. I've never seen myself working in an office." This was the man Devlin would like to have been had he been a real living man and not a figure attached to the dirty imaginings of the itinerant female, Las Vegas Tajay.

* * *

On its website the FBI requests that victims of these catfish scams report the details to them. I have had mixed dealings with the Bureau over the years, according to a file about me released in the 1980s. As I recall, they had begun a file about me in the 1960s. I was enrolled in the brand-new Ph.D. program at the City University of New York that was established only the year before I arrived, which was in 1962. My friend Pat Moriarity and I were interested in writing, in the romance of writing. So, one Saturday morning found us at a writers' conference at the downtown Brooklyn campus of Long Island University.

The speakers were the British playwright John Arden, and French novelists Michel Butor, who had written a novel in the second person; Natalie Sarraute and Claude Simon. The French carried the day. There was no politics other than literary experimentation. I don't remember who represented the United States. Vietnam was not yet our preoccupation and a necessary subject of our discourse. That was soon to change.

When we returned from lunch, there was a sheet of paper placed face up on each chair. It announced the formation of a FREE UNIVERSITY OF NEW YORK at a building on East 14th Street with an array of courses in the arts and politics. We were not surprised or put off. We were willing to study *Beowulf* and *The Faerie Queen*, Wordsworth and Coleridge, John Ruskin, and Virginia Woolf, but not only these eminences of the British Empire. The CUNY curriculum felt stifling, although we were not ready or coherent enough to articulate that complaint.

I enrolled in a course in the early writings of Karl Marx, taught by an adjunct professor at Drew University named Jim Mellen. I duly read everything placed before me. Eventually I taught some courses in literary topics myself. My movements were recorded by the doorman of the building where I lived, 2 Washington Square Village. He was a tall, dark, pleasant fellow and told the Bureau that I was "attractive." This surprised me. Was he talking about *me*? The file was scant, reflecting that I was, in those years, so shy that I rarely talked to anyone.

I never realized that the FBI's COINTELPRO representative at the Free University was one Leonard Liggio. Tall and stout, dressed always in a black trench coat, dark suit and tie, Leonard was everybody's favorite uncle. Leonard was entirely non-judgmental, saying little, but always present, even as he lived somewhere in the Bronx with his mother, which was all we knew. He turned out to be part of the legitimizing landscape, until his true identity was exposed.

Leonard Liggio and the Free U faded from my life, but the FBI remained a presence. In attempting to research the JFK assassination, like everyone else, I was subjected to the FBI's redactions, only, abruptly, for their mood to change. Not that taking Jim Garrison as a biographical subject was a felicitous choice.

I had discussed the situation with my friend Charlie Ellis, CEO of John Wiley publishers. "I think you should reconsider," Charlie said at once. "This could ruin your career." The year was 1997. Garrison was persona non grata everywhere from the CIA to the *New York Times*. Garrison had become convinced that Lee Harvey Oswald was not a shooter on November 22, 1963, no matter what the Warren Commission and the *New York Times* alleged. I, who had grown up believing that the *New York Times* was always right, took a deep breath.

Charlie's invocation of the term "career" had startled me. Still, I thought of Charlie Ellis as a morally vacant person who prioritized money and status. (*Publisher's Weekly* put his annual salary in the high six figures.) I never considered Wiley as a potential publisher of a book about Garrison.

Nor would I offer it to the publisher of my biography of Kay Boyle, Roger Straus, with his admitted service to CIA which he outlined to me one hot summer day on the veranda of his mansion in Purchase, New York.

By the 2000s, without warning, the FBI began to send me requested documents with fewer redactions. Our relationship seemed almost harmonious. Researching a Texan named Malcolm Wallace, supposedly a surrogate for Lyndon Johnson in his non-existent participation in the Kennedy assassination, I had made a FOIA request for an unredacted copy of Wallace's original FBI file, one that had been so splashed with inky black splatter that you could scarcely read any of it.

The Bureau replied in record time, sending me a virtually clean file. This was immensely helpful, as I acknowledged in my book about the Malcolm Wallace story. Wallace, I discovered, had nothing to do with the murder of President Kennedy. The book was called *Faustian Bargains*, and you will find the FBI among the acknowledgments.

My greatest helper in attempting to uncover the roots and causes of the assassination was the aforementioned New Orleans police officer, Robert Buras. Retired now, Bob had been a young policeman walking the beat in the French Quarter when Jim Garrison took office as district attorney. As such, he attempted to eliminate corruption from the bars and other establishments on Bourbon Street and environs. Buras moved on to police intelligence, then to the House Select Committee on Assassinations in the late seventies.

In a landscape riddled with corruption, Robert Buras was unique: he was an honest man. His help to me was invaluable. I wrote him so many emails with questions that he took to addressing me as "Dear Sherlock." That he lacked a fancy formal education did not mean that Bob was a stranger to irony. He, of course, was the "Sherlock," a connoisseur of investigations, I the bumbling, grateful amateur. Put it this way. Robert Buras was the Larry Bird of police work. Brilliant minds in different fields. Formal education had nothing to do with it in either case.

I had one further encounter with the FBI. In a radio interview, I did many in those years, I was asked about Roger Stone's diatribe, *The Man Who Killed Kennedy: The Case Against LBJ* (2014). I remarked that there was no evidence whatsoever that placed Johnson as the organizer or a participant in the president's murder. There was simply no documentation of the book's central assertion. There are a handful of endnotes in Stone's book, but these are to secondary sources, other people's work.

I soon heard from Stone himself in a phone call that terrified me. "I see that you are scheduled to speak in New Orleans at a conference about the Kennedy assassination," Stone began. This was true. My topic was Jim Garrison and my book, *A Farewell to Justice*.

"Should you attend that meeting," Stone threatened, "you will come to bodily harm, and I will also sue you." Stone and Donald Trump were both protégés of the infamous Roy Cohn and both would later be connected to Proud Boys' leader, Enrique Tarrio. It was said that Stone

served as an intermediary between Tarrio and Donald Trump as they organized the events of January 6th, 2021. Tarrio was ultimately convicted of sedition and sentenced to twenty-two years in prison.

Calling himself a "dirty trickster," Stone wanted you to fear him. Few, if any, of the JFK assassination researchers had the courage to challenge Stone's theory about Lyndon Johnson's role in the murder. So he sprinkled fear over the fragile JFK assassination literary landscape. Terror was his modus operandi.

Convicted of seven counts of malfeasance, Stone was scheduled to begin serving a forty-month prison sentence. Donald Trump granted him a full pardon on July 10, 2020. Wiped from existence was the $20,000 fine that he would never pay.

Trump argued that Stone could not possibly be expected to serve his sentence while the corona virus roared its way through the prison system. You can perceive the ghost of Roy Cohn's mentor, Senator Joseph McCarthy, prowling among the living, impatient to bear witness to the long-awaited fall of Democracy.

Stone said that he preferred his sentence be commuted (rather than that he be pardoned) so that he could request a new trial to clear his name. The day after Stone was pardoned and his sentence was commuted, Robert Mueller, prosecutor of the investigation of Trump's alliance with the Russians, wrote an op ed arguing that Stone remained a "convicted felon and rightly so." It was now that Stone dubbed himself a "dirty trickster," a warning to anyone who might oppose him. Then, yes, I did fear him.

Stone's subpoena from the House Committee investigating the January 6th insurrection reads, "You were there," as he was, surrounded by bodyguards from a militia group, The Oath Keepers.

Frightened by Stone's threats, I telephoned my lawyer, a New Jersey stalwart. "Never mention his name again!" John Saxon advised. Roger Stone's sleazy quasi-terrorism was beyond Saxon's experience, even as the country's steady descent into fascism was becoming familiar to us all.

I thought I might consult the Bureau for its view, but really its protection, and so I attempted to look up the FBI field office closest to me. (The FBI has field offices throughout the country, each with a Special Agent in Charge [SAC], as well as plain Special Agents, some of whom I had discovered were better at their jobs than the SAC. Such was the case in New Orleans where Warren de Brueys was the FBI agent nonpareil. Among those assigned to Mr. de Brueys was Lee Harvey Oswald. Of course, when I asked Mr. de Brueys about this, he flashed a wicked smile. "That's far-fetched," he said. But he didn't deny it. It would take a Warren de Brueys to gain an edge over Roger Stone.)

When I called the Newark field office of the Bureau, they directed me to the Resident Agent in Trenton.

A kindly woman, a female agent I was pleased to hear, since the many FBI agents I met during my investigation of the Garrison investigation were all male, listened to what I had to say. She was quiet, then promised to call me back. A week later she telephoned. "He works for Trump," she said. Nothing more needed to be said.

"I just want Stone's threats to be on the record," I said. "I'm not asking for anything."

"When I landed at Louis Armstrong Airport in New Orleans, I was met by the conference organizer. I told him that I had reported Stone's threats to the FBI. Surely even Roger Stone, knowing that the FBI was watching, would pause before sending some stray bully to greet me with "bodily harm," as he put it. That was my strategy, to let Stone know we were under surveillance. It turned out that he was not ready to cast the rule of law aside. It worked.

The conference organizer had published a book of mine, *Our Man in Haiti*, its focus one of Oswald's Dallas CIA handlers, George de Mohrenschildt. The next glitch was that although I had informed the organizers that I was disabled and required a room near the conference events, that room had been given away to someone else. The sleazy hotel was on a strip of highway outside New Orleans. A conference sponsor was a woman whose claim to fame was a sexual relationship with Lee Harvey Oswald. The main event was a birthday party for Oswald. I did not attend. Among the 1200 people I had interviewed for *A Farewell to Justice*, no one had heard of her.

Looking back, I must record that the assassination research "community" had lacked the courage to dismiss Roger Stone's unsupported book accusing Lyndon Johnson of being the mastermind of the Kennedy assassination. They had responded to Stone's invasion of their precincts with a catatonia that bespoke fear. At their conferences, and in their websites, Stone was rarely mentioned, as if he were a magical being. The significant exception was an indomitable woman who went by the tag "JFK Annie." Her real name is Andrea Skolnick.

I gave my talk about Jim Garrison without incident. All the seats were occupied, which was gratifying. Roger Stone was not present in the room, nor did I attend his meeting that afternoon. I was told that he had promised his audience he would sue me for $42,000. From whence that figure derived, I have no idea. Perhaps it was what Stone believed he could extract from a shabby, aging college professor residing in rural New Jersey, the way Tajay [Devlin's partner] had settled on $15,000 as what they could extort from a catfished intellectual.

Allow me to mention that Roger Stone was not the only person who threatened to sue me for my writing. In the late 1970s I worked on a story that would be published as a true crime book called *Privilege*. At the center of the story was a young woman named "Sasha Bruce." When I asked her mother for an interview, she told me to go to Washington D.C. to meet with her lawyer, Edward Bennett Williams.

As I struggled to find the conference room, I passed a gigantic television set, and it came to me that he was a part owner of the Washington Redskins football team, now the Commanders.

A red-faced, stout Williams flung himself into a chair. He had only one message for me, and it had nothing to do with organizing an interview with Evangeline Bruce. If I used a

Sherlock at a Temple University gathering for creative writers, with John Banville the Irish novelist, circa 2000.

single word from the *Life* magazine article about Sasha's death, Williams sputtered, he would sue me. The erosion of the first amendment began long before the advent of Donald Trump.

There are people who can control what is published about them and Evangeline Bruce considered herself one of them. Later Mrs. Bruce went to New York where she appeared at the offices of The Dial Press, which was still on schedule to publish my book.

"John," Mrs. Bruce said to the editor-in-chief, John Sargent, "you're not going to publish that book, are you?" Dial/Doubleday did publish *Privilege*, even as neither the words "Sasha" nor "Bruce" appeared anywhere on the jacket, but without any support. Soon there was a flood in the warehouse and the existing stock of books vanished, never to be replaced. I showed *Privilege* to an acquaintance, Kurt Vonnegut. He called it a "swell book."

My intention had been to write a sympathetic book about Sasha Bruce, who was my contemporary, and to examine whether her bountiful privilege had been of any service to her in her effort to devise an authentic life. Certainly, it led European fortune hunters to her door. These characters bore no resemblance to the rich and handsome, if bland, men of her youth whom she had encountered on Mount Desert Island, in Maine where the rich gather during the summer vacations.

I met Sasha's friends such as Wendy Wisner, daughter of the CIA legend Frank Wisner. I did receive a blurb for the paperback of *Privilege*, from Benjamin Bradlee, the executive editor of the *Washington Post*, who turned out to be a supporter of freedom of expression. I was snubbed by Mrs. Bruce's friend, Arthur Schlesinger, who was not.

A coda to this story. Years later, when I was writing about the intelligence services, I came upon references to the "Bruce-Lovett Report." Sasha's Ambassador father, David K. E. Bruce, had been commissioned by President Eisenhower to write an assessment of CIA's clandestine services. By the mid-1950's, the CIA was already in moral disarray, but the Agency managed to destroy every extant copy of the Bruce-Lovett report.

Nor was it only the CIA that interfered with American literary efforts. A dramatist named John Hadden Jr., son of a lifetime CIA officer, had trouble finding a publisher for his memoir, *Conversations with a Masked Man*. He wound up with Arcade Books, a nondescript house created by Richard Seaver and his wife Jeannette. Seaver had run Grove Press in its heyday. A friendly Mossad asset related to young Hadden that he had remarked upon the publication of Hadden's *Conversations with a Masked Man* to former Mossad director Efraim Halevy.

"I thought we had taken care of that!" Halevy said.

* * *

Roger Stone did not make good on his threat. He did not sue me in any court of law. He had no credible proof that LBJ murdered John F. Kennedy, with or without the assistance of Malcolm Wallace. We had not yet been liberated from the rule of law. Unfortunately, it is not a crime to lie. You can accuse anyone of killing JFK, and the law will not come knocking at your door. This has been demonstrated by the exposure of Trump and David Pecker of the *National Enquirer*, who accused Ted Cruz's father of being involved in the JFK assassination.

I turned one final time to the FBI. On its website, there is a category called "romantic scams," which have been elevated to the status of crimes. There is a form directed to the Bureau reporting on what had happened to you [the victim]. I did complete this form, with special emphasis on the particulars of Tajay Edgerson. After all, by now I was not sure that a Michael Devlin had ever been writing to me.

The Bureau did not reply. I was disappointed, but I understood. Catfishing had reached epidemic proportions. Tajay and Devlin had not extracted a dollar of my money. Other victims had been stripped of upwards of $100,000. They were more deserving of the FBI's attention. I never met either Devlin or Tajay. I don't need to see them now, whomever they may be. I have resisted the temptation of contacting Nev and Kamie at the *Catfish: The TV Show*.

In a world where selfishness is rampant, their motive should have been obvious—at least from the moment money was mentioned. In a society where objective truth is no longer acknowledged as real, people and their feelings no longer exist. It is a disservice to the victims that the *Catfish* program promotes forgiveness, as if the harm inflicted on the victims was not significant or permanent. The Netflix Manti documentary says otherwise. At the close of that film, Manti remains a broken man.

* * *

I am reminded of the ending of the great Japanese director Shohei Imamura's film, *The Pornographers* (1966). A man who has encountered his share of life's troubles falls in love with a life-sized rubber doll in whose solitary company he sets sail in a small boat into Tokyo Bay. Perhaps you've wondered: how can you fall head over heels in love with someone you've never met and whose voice you've never heard?

Sherlock with Coach Bob Knight at left, Bloomington, Indiana, 1988. At right is assistant coach Ron Felling.

You can drift off to oblivion just as a rubber doll can curl up in your heart. Secure in his love, it represents no sacrifice for Imamura's character to have left his messy Tokyo life behind. Devlin might have been just such a rubber doll, or not existed at all, even as he remains real to me, an ideal of my own creation, a lost promise. As Manti discovered, this is what happens when you open your heart.

I was never even to work out the clue that his failure to telephone suggested, that the person to whom I was writing was of the wrong gender, like the catfish tormenting Manti, a transgender woman. On *Catfish*, Nev remarks, "You can't trust anyone on the Internet," The kindly co-host Max adds, "The older you are, the bigger the scar it leaves."

One of the victims, a rapper named "Prophet," says matter-of-factly, "You can be anybody on the Internet." You don't know to whom you're talking, male or female, a high school student or a grizzled outlier. It can be a nihilist or, on the rare occasion, a compassionate soul. Few of the catfish can register the harm they have done. Their lives are entirely about themselves. They feel nothing for their victims, who are as unreal to them as their own contrived and shifting identities.

The catfish exposed by Nev Schulman and Max Joseph in the early seasons of *Catfish* are invariably grotesquely overweight and lacking in self-confidence. They whine about the hard lot life has dealt them. "No one ever cared about me," several catfish complain. "Sometimes I don't feel good about myself," one says.

Universally, their education is scanty. Self-education, studying, and hard labor are foreign to them. You don't want to know them. Caught in the act, their mantra is, "I'm sorry. I didn't mean to hurt anyone." Every one of these apologies is worthless. Sometimes they offer a variation on "I felt like being somebody else." Then, they turn themselves into victims. They were bullied, they lost their parents at a young age, no one loved them. Always the catfish becomes indignant at being called a liar.

As Max says in one of his last appearances on *Catfish*, "Who knows what's real and what's fake anymore?" In the email where Devlin claimed he was so overcome with passion that he felt as if he had fallen into a canyon, the voice had changed; it was not the same person. I am appalled now that I didn't foresee what was coming.

* * *

As in the unforgettable Hollywood films of the 1930s and 1940s, the pages of a calendar fall inexorably to the floor. The telephone rings. A male voice.

"Hello, Joan," it says slowly, as if it had all the time in the world. "This is Michael Devlin." He uses the word "respect," a concept no Catfish understands. Is this the man with the small grey goatee depicted in that photograph at the helm of a logging machine deep in some unidentifiable forest?

I have no idea. I listen for a foreign accent, even as our reverse image search located his logging machine with its wide picture window to have originated somewhere in Romania. Unlike many exposed catfish, he never admitted that he lied, so I ended up not ever knowing to whom I was talking.

Yes, this was a dream. There never was, nor would there ever be, any such telephone call.

* * *

It is August 14 in my eternal year 2023. During a New York Mets baseball game, the superlative broadcaster Gary Cohen compares an Atlanta Braves player to Paul Bunyan, a "lumberjack," and my heart skips a beat. Former Mets star Keith Hernandez notes that the Mets owner has suddenly sold off his two star players, Max Scherzer and Justin Verlander, and compares this destruction of the team to a "demolition."

Everything is about money, and money cancels out all else. A hedge-fund billionaire has no business running a baseball team any more than a real-life logger could connect with a New York Jewish intellectual. But in the world as it has come to be, the billionaire can treat two athletes of great accomplishment as if they were pawns in the 19th century slave trade.

Had it not all been a con, he would have found me by now. And yet the Devlin in the photos had himself been a victim. His identity had been appropriated so that he had no idea of who I was. He had never heard of me. The secret would remain, the final sadistic touch, revenge for my never sending them any money.

This is a cruel game, a travesty, and a sin. "You're probably hurt," one catfish says on the TV series. "But I'm hurt more." Another catfish says, "everything was true, except the physicality." You have to laugh at that. "It's all a game," a catfish attempts to cover up what surely should count as a crime ... like playing a part in a movie." Self-centeredness, "individuality," the raw ugliness of "self" have taken over.

Had there been a "real" Michael Devlin, I would have packed up all my worldly goods and moved in with him. But I would like to think not.

* * *

The summer of 2023 melted into history, taking with it my desire for this trickster, Michael Devlin. What I did not anticipate coming to pass was that Ralph would die. He died in July, leaving me alone and without his constancy, forever.

Sherlock at Barnes & Noble in Rittenhouse Square, Philadelphia, Pennsylvania, 2006.

The incandescent days of this golden autumn drew to a close with the cruelties of the war in Israel. Worst of all was the news on November 30th that for a year the government of Israel held a blueprint of the October 7 Hamas attacks on Israel. So, and all the media have agreed, the murders, torture, and kidnappings could have been prevented. This involved the taking of hostages, including babies and the very old. The sailors of the USS *Liberty* were all innocents too, as CIA and the Mossad put their lives in jeopardy.

Always, with unconditional aid from the United States, Israel maintained its well-oiled military apparatus. At once they turned residential Gaza into a field of rubble. Caught red-handed, the Israelis claimed the Hamas plans were "aspirational," whatever that means. Then they added as an excuse for not acting on the purloined plans that were in their hands for over a year that they didn't believe Hamas were capable of such attacks.

The responses of the Israeli government defy what we know of Mossad's capabilities and the quality of the intelligence they gather. Meanwhile, on the West Bank settlers roam killing people and sheep and other animals. Move out, the Palestinians are ordered as their enemies laugh behind their hands. This is ethnic cleansing. "You shouldn't have looked," Gerald Patrick Hemming liked to say. What went on in Gaza and the West Bank applies.

I wrote a book about collaboration between the Israeli state, the Mossad, and the CIA called *Blood In The Water*, thus increasing my familiarity with such operations. Rendering Gaza unlivable, with no concern for its displaced and homeless residents, Israel resumed its attack.

Aware of the difficulty of how to create a free and peaceful Palestinian state, the Palestinians who had the money have sent their children to the best American universities, such as Brown, Haverford or Trinity (Connecticut). A striking example was the splendid three students wearing their keffiyeh scarves who were shot in Burlington, Vermont on Thanksgiving of 2023.

"Murder wol out," wrote the great English poet Geoffrey Chaucer. The facts will come out. Hadn't Jim Garrison said the same thing with respect to the Kennedy assassination? MSNBC's *Morning Joe* tried to rationalize the facts that were emerging. But what are we to make of this program with its CIA imprint in the persons of frequent guests like Robert Hass, retired president of the New York branch of the Council on Foreign Relations. This entity was founded by CIA eminence Allen Dulles himself. For a time, Dulles even received his personal mail there.

Discussing the current Israeli war, one day the hosts of *Morning Joe* enlisted the meaningless word "conspiracy," only at once to banish that buzzword from all further discussions of the Hamas war. Did the revelation that the Israeli government had in hand for more than a year in advance maps of the October 7 attacks mean that there had been a conspiracy between Israel and Hamas? Did it mean that in its silence Israel condoned the atrocities against Israeli women and children as the price they were willing to pay for ridding the land once and for all of its original inhabitants? The process seemed indeed like "ethnic cleansing." Nor did

Morning Joe return to the issue of an investigation of the foreknowledge the Israeli government possessed a year in advance of the Hamas attacks, as they had promised. The Israeli government did not deny that they were in possession of this material.

The blueprint seen by the Israelis was 40 pages long. There were signals intelligence, and evidence of Hamas fighters practicing in training camps for the supposedly surprise attacks of October 7. I could see in these blueprints the signature of the Mossad, which I studied for *Blood in the Water* published in 2018. The *New York Times* referred to this information as originating from "intelligence services."

The chief intelligence officer on the *Liberty*, Dave Lewis, had recruited me to write a book about the *Liberty*. God rest Mr. Lewis's soul, and "flights of angels sing thee to thy rest." Mr. Lewis read my manuscript and suggested changes. He read it at least three times. By the time the book was published, he had become my closest friend.

The notion that there was no collusion between the state of Israel and Hamas is unthinkable. What was Israel's motive? How did the Netanyahu perspective allow the Israeli state to hurt so many of its own people? It had to be what it has always been – the ethnic cleansing of the land dating from 1948 to rid it of as many Palestinians (with no right to return!) as possible and so solve the problem of unhappy, disgruntled Palestinians longing for equality under the law and living too close for comfort. Ralph always opposed the "two states" solution. He was for equality with Palestinians living in the state of Israel as equal citizens.

* * *

As for Michael Devlin, Audrey dismisses him now as an AI generated creature, another rubber doll, the spawn of a soulless algorithm following a script, not a human being at all.

You might wonder what forces had left me so vulnerable that even when I knew better, I succumbed. In truth, had I given Devlin the opportunity to ask, I would have given him not only the $15,000 he requested, but every cent I had accumulated over my lifetime. As may seem obvious I could not forgive myself for letting him into my life. Even now, so many years later, I do not believe I was worthy of survival, my mother and brother both having already gone down under the sadism and brutality of the man who tormented us every day of our lives. Laughing hysterically, he would sometimes call himself a "Dr. Jekyll and Mr. Hyde."

I had been a secret participant and enabler because I knew deep within me that I would escape my father. At the age of nineteen I was finally able to get away. I could not, during all the years that followed, forgive myself for witnessing what he did and not being able to do anything about it, for myself, or anyone else. I still needed to be punished. I was not worthy of living a normal life, and, yes, of being loved.

Hating myself, feeling I deserved to be treated this way because of the lasting damage my father had inflicted with his cruelty, this was my legacy. After Ralph, I never would be loved again, although I could write this tale. I learned to hate myself too long ago for that to change. I was a perfect victim of what NYU psychiatrist Leonard Sheingold termed "Soul Murder."

Cervantes closes his story with the word VALE, which means "Farewell." Like the knight errant, I also have had enough. Like Herman Melville's Ishmael, I alone survived to tell this tale of having endured the unthinkable. "VALE" is what you say when you are utterly worn out.

And it is still – or so it seems – only 1605

NOTES

For the subversion of MFA programs by CIA beginning after World War Two, see Eric Bennett, *Workshops of Empire: Stegner, Engle and American Creative Writing During the Cold War*, (University of Iowa Press: Iowa City, 2015). This remarkable book exposes CIA's efforts to fashion cold war intellectuals through humanities departments and the creative writing programs that proliferated in the fifties and sixties and beyond.

Steve Almond, "Write an essay," See Bennett, p, 272.

The catfishing manual from Nigeria, quoted by Dr. Phil, is titled "How to Make a White Woman Fall In Love With You." It is available online from Online Chat. Forty pages. The pseudonymous author acknowledges that he is Nigerian. On the cover of this pamphlet an interracial couple embraces while they are being showered by twenty-dollar bills in US currency.

The Tinder Swindler and *The Girlfriend Who Didn't Exist* are both available on NETFLIX.

Roger Stone and Enrique Tarrio, "Former Leader of Proud Boys Says Prosecutors Sought a Link to Trump," by Alan Feuer. *New York Times*, September 9, 2023, p. A15.

The story of the origin of the term "catfishing" is recounted in a documentary feature length film by Nev Schulman and is available on MTV, carried by the HULU network. Dr. Phil (CBS Network TV) does the subject a service by including in his programing many middle-aged and older women who are more likely victims of catfishing. The 18-24 age group are more fiercely canny, and less likely to be hoodwinked.

They are also less likely to possess quantities of ready cash to be wired to the catfish.

The story of Florentino Ariza and Fermina Daza is told in Gabriel García Márquez, *Love in The Time of Cholera*, (Alfred A. Knopf, 1988). It is, in my humble estimation, the greatest love story ever written, not least because García Márquez, humane soul that he was, believed in love. I interviewed García Márquez in Mexico City in 1984. He was a warm, kindly man, as perplexed about why people do what they do as any one of us.

Our subject was his college classmate, Father Camilo Torres Restrepo, who left the priesthood to join the ELN, a Colombian guerrilla group, in 1966. It seems apparent that Camilo was placed in harm's way by the leader of the group, Fabio Vásquez Castaño. Officially, Camilo was murdered by a marauding Army patrol. For an account of the death of Father Camilo Torres Restrepo, see Jaime Arenas Reyes, *La Guerrilla Por Dentro*. Tercer Mundo, Tercer Edición. Bogotá, Colombia. 1971, In Spanish.

Rashomon: A film by Akira Kurosawa. Grove Press, Inc., New York. 1969. The script is here along with many photographs and supporting materials, including the Akutagawa stories upon which the film was based.

Cristina Garcia's most recent novel is *Vanishing Maps* (Alfred A. Knopf, 2023).

The planet Tralfamadore appears in Kurt Vonnegut's *Slaughterhouse-Five or The Children's Crusade, or, A Duty-Dance with Death*. (A Dial Press Trade Paperback, 2009).

For the Israel-Hamas war, see, for example, "Israel Saw Hamas Attack Plan a Year Ago but Dismissed It as Undoable," *New York Times*, December 1, 2023, pp. A1, A9. See also, David Shulman, "A Bitter Season in the West Bank," *The New York Review of Books*, December 21, 2023. pp. 20-22.

Patrick Kingsley and Aaron Boxerman, "Israeli Officers' Errors Draw Scrutiny, but Little Backlash," *New York Times*,

December 3, 2023, p. 13.; Michael L. "What Israel Owes the Palestinians of Gaza." *New York Times*, Sunday Opinion," December 3, 2023. P. 4.

"VALE" is the final word in Miguel de Cervantes' *Don Quijote de la Mancha*. (1605). Like the feisty knight errant, and close to being as worn out, I have had enough.

For further discussion of the Israel-Hamas war, please refer to Ilan Pappe's speech before the student body at the University of California, Berkeley, on October 19, 2023, YouTube. Thank you to Jeffrey Mackler. See also: Megan K. Stack, "They Terrorize us at Night, Send Messages to Leave the Village," *New York Times*, Opinion Section. December 10, 2023. P. 6. See also: Mark Mazzetti and Ronen Bergman, "Israel Long Let Cash from Qatar Prop up Hamas," *New York Times*, December 10, 2023, p. 1; 12. See also: "Crisis in Palestine," https://consortiumnews.com/2023/10/23/watch

"U.S. Wants Israel to Scale Down Attack in Gaza as Civilian Toll Grows," *New York Times*, December 15, 2023. A1, A6.

"Israel Got Secret Hamas Ledgers but Didn't Halt Flow of Funds," *New York Times*, December 17, 2023, p. 10. "UN Resolution Does Little for Gaza Without Truce, Aid Groups Say," *New York Times*, December 24, 2023, p. A8.

See also Masha Gessen, "In the Shadow of the Holocaust." *The New Yorker*. https://www.newyorker.com/news/the-weekend-essay/in-the-shadow-of-the-holocaust

Index

T

U

V

W